Happiness that

To dear Garry
with love &
gratitude for all
your help & advice
and - moreover -
your friendship
Linda & John.

Other books by Martin Israel include:

Summons to Life (Mowbray)
Precarious Living (Mowbray)
Smouldering Fire (Mowbray)
The Spirit of Counsel (Mowbray)
Dark Victory (Mowbray)
Doubt: The Way of Growth (Mowbray)

Living Alone (SPCK)
The Pearl of Great Price (SPCK)
Night Thoughts (SPCK)
Life Eternal (SPCK)
The Quest for Wholeness (Darton, Longman & Todd)
Light on the Path (Darton, Longman & Todd)
The Pain That Heals (Arthur James)

Happiness that Lasts

Martin Israel

CASSELL

Cassell
Wellington House, 125 Strand, London WC2R 0BB
370 Lexington Avenue, New York, NY 10017–6550
www.cassell.co.uk

© Martin Israel 1999
www.martinisrael.com

First published 1999

British Library Cataloguing-in Publication Data
A catalogue record for this book is available from the British Library.

ISBN 0–304–70242–0

Biblical quotations are taken from the Revised English Bible,
© Oxford University Press and Cambridge University Press, 1989

Typeset by Ensystems, Saffron Walden, Essex
Printed and bound in Great Britain by Biddles Ltd,
Guildford & Kings Lynn

Contents

To Rupert

Introduction

Tyger, tyger, burning bright
In the forests of the night,
What immortal hand or eye
Could frame thy fearful symmetry?

In what distant deeps or skies,
Burnt the fire of thine eyes?
On what wings dare he aspire?
What the hand dare seize the fire?

And what shoulder & what art,
Could twist the sinews of thy heart?
And, when thy heart began to beat,
What dread hand & what dread feet?

What the hammer? What the chain?
In what furnace was thy brain?
What the anvil? What dread grasp
Dare its deadly terrors clasp?

When the stars threw down their spears,
And water'd heaven with their tears,
Did He smile His work to see?
Did He who made the lamb make thee?

Tyger, tyger, burning bright
In the forests of the night,
What immortal hand or eye
Dare frame thy fearful symmetry?
    (William Blake, *Songs of Experience*)

Happiness is a universal need, and at the same time the
purpose of our life. If people could be really happy, there

would be no ill-will, because they would be satisfied with their present condition. It therefore follows that happiness is closely allied to contentment. But what makes a person happy? I have little doubt that if the mass of humanity were asked that question, a number of views would emerge. It is probable that first on the list would be having more money, followed by a position of sufficient power to control their own lives (and also surreptitiously the lives of others).

Those with more experience would see that health was the most important prerequisite for happiness, and I do not think that anyone with common sense could deny this. The problem here is how to attain and maintain this health. So often it appears to be an illusion, and, indeed, the nature of life itself with the frailty of the human body makes this an inevitable concomitant of our incarnation. Some of a quieter, more profound disposition would see friendship as an essential part of happiness. This friendship may have sexual or family overtones, but in the end there is a mutual benevolence that is independent of even these two vital constituents. Others would see love as the full achievement of happiness, and few would dispute the accuracy of that observation, and indeed it is the third of the theological virtues praised in 1 Corinthians 13:13. The snag here, however, is the multi-dimensional character of what we call love – it ranges in breadth from sexual desire (not so far removed sometimes from undisguised lust) to a warm-hearted concern and self-giving for all people.

How is this achieved? Love is in fact an act of the will, but it is not the egoistical will at all so much as the will of God, whose nature is always to have love, acting through our own little wills. It is very hard to give ourselves over absolutely to God's love, because this may necessitate a descent into darkness. Indeed, I would insist that such a descent is essential if we are to know the loving nature of God, because while I, as a person, take precedence, God himself is occluded from my sight. Therefore darkness, even up to temporary despair, may be an essential staging post in our journey to happiness, but if we persist to the end the iridescence of joy will make itself known to us, and it will be made lasting through the ever-increasing warmth of happiness.

This progress from the indifferent, rather selfish life of the man or woman in the street to those who know happiness is not a particularly easy or pleasant one, but I have no doubt that it is the authentic way. It was not for nothing that Moses and the children of Israel had to traverse the wilderness for forty years before they reached the frontier of the Promised Land – and poor Moses himself was not allowed to enter because in some undisclosed way he had displeased God. Jeremiah, possibly the greatest of the writing prophets, was confirmed in the truth of his prophecy by his total rejection at the hands of the Israelites, who carried him forcibly with them into Egypt; they themselves, and presumably Jeremiah also, were all destroyed by King Nebuchadnezzar, who hailed from Babylon.

In the much more apocryphal story of Job, he too had to be deprived of all earthly possessions and even his own health before the lingering shreds of his egoistical pride could be removed. The greatest of all the stories of suffering as a necessary precursor of happiness, however, is seen in the life of Jesus; though without sin he followed the course of any other man; though he gave of himself heart and soul to all who sought his help, he was despised and rejected by all people as the Jews themselves engineered his execution at the hands of Pontius Pilate and his Roman soldiers. In the end, he was resurrected, and the completion of his story has been one of personal triumph and some degree of civilization of those who claim to follow his path.

How many real Christians there are is another matter entirely. As Madame Roland (1754–93) said with regard to the French Revolution: 'Oh Liberty! Oh Liberty! What crimes are committed in thy name!'

It seems evident from this initial meditation that merely possessing the things of this world will not produce anything more than a fleeting happiness: the world goes on, even if we get stuck on a particularly delightful present moment.

Happiness that lasts

None of the earlier prerequisites for happiness that I have already mentioned are necessarily illusory, but in themselves they cannot help but be evanescent. The value of them paradoxically is to prove their transitory nature, and how neutral they are in our own lives. This applies even to health inasmuch as it may be that chronic disablement is our way forward to attaining inner peace.

> I strove with none; for none was worth my strife;
> Nature I loved, and, next to Nature, Art;
> I warmed both hands before the fire of life;
> It sinks, and I am ready to depart.
> (*Finis, Epigrams* c *Death*. Walter Savage Landor (1775–1864))

1 The darkness inherent in life

Nothing changes one's attitude to life more radically than sudden dramatic adversity. Black may seem more like white, while tragedy may open out a previously restricted personality into one of enormous potentiality. During the past year my life has been completely transformed. I now look at life in a different way.

Return from the portals of death

In recent times an increasingly large literature has appeared on the transition between life and death. In near-death experiences, after a variable period of completely altered consciousness the person returns to awareness and gives a dramatic account of what was experienced during the period of apparent bliss. I must confess that sometimes the descriptions have appeared slightly too dramatic, though this may merely be professional jealousy on my part. However, during the last eight months I have had a quite dramatic episode of completely altered consciousness, which was in no way blissful or inflating, but rather brought me to the solid portals of death. This is the account of the occurrence which I have tried to make as accurate as I can, while acknowledging that I can remember little of it myself, but have had to rely totally on the accounts of a highly trustworthy carer and some friends.

We start our life in a state of complete ignorance (the so-called *tabula rasa* of the philosophers) but as our years proceed, so more and more knowledge accrues to us. The most important understanding consists in coming to terms more fully with our own personality, and being able to see ourselves in truth without the need for prevarication. This is seldom an especially enjoyable exposure, but as we proceed, so we become increasingly adult in our relationships with other people and more acceptable to society as a whole. There does come a time when we have to face the fact that our life's work has been largely completed and our body is beginning to fail. This is a much more important experience than the outgoing extroversion of youth, when so much valuable constructive work is being done. As we grow older, so we have to draw in our horns and realize that our really great work in life is the development of our character and our capacity to be of help to other people. No matter how important we may have been in our place, we have to yield with gentle courtesy and give that place to those who are younger and more eligible than we are. The end of this process is quite obviously death, which at a certain stage is not only essential for our own development, but also for that of those who are destined to follow on where we have been obliged to fall away. To most people this is the tragedy of life, but the wise ones welcome it with increasing acceptance as they become older and more frail.

Age, in fact, has solid virtues; it deadens any tendency we might have had to sins of personal gratification, and the fatigue that is a part of ageing makes the future much more tolerable. We realize that death and sleep are fairly closely related and we can relax gently into the quietness of slumber with joy, 'How wonderful is Death, Death and his brother Sleep!' (Shelley, 'Queen Mab').

If one is really determined in one's quest for happiness, it is not sufficient merely to have overcome worldly temptations and conditions that we shall subsequently consider; one also has to experience at first hand the darkness, indeed, the terrors inherent in life itself. It was not for nothing that Jesus counselled the rich young man who came to him asking what he should do in order to possess eternal life to get rid of all his possessions and give the money to the poor, even though he had previously lived irreproachably. On one level this simply means that one should not cling on to anything whatsoever if one is to know the ultimate truth, but in fact the circumstances of life will reduce one progressively to one's own true stature and remove any source of attachment from everything. Buddhism is particularly strict in its demand for austerity in the matter of clinging on to anything in this world. In the episode recounted in Matthew 19: 16–22 when the young man is counselled to sell his possessions and give to the poor, he goes away sad, for he was a man of great wealth. I doubt quite candidly whether anybody could have followed Jesus' counsel directly; as we shall see when we consider wealth in Chapter 2, even those who enter a religious community have the necessities for reasonable living at their disposal. However, what Jesus was prescribing for the young man was a complete renunciation of all worldly goods; only then could he follow Jesus and what he stood for. In fact, this crucial piece of advice is not something we choose, but rather something that befalls us when we, like Job, are suddenly reduced to absolute poverty and affliction for no apparent fault of our own: only then can we come to reality. At last we remember that we were born out of nothing and that when we die we will again be nothing in the world's eyes, even if our immediate death causes great mourning. Death is itself a mystery, and no scheme of survival that humans have devised is anything more than conjectural.

It would be most helpful to describe my own experience of outer darkness. I mention in Chapter 7 that I was received into the Anglican Church in 1971. Four years later I was ordained priest and I spent the following 22 years in parish ministry, while pursuing retreat conducting, exorcism, healing work and writing a considerable number of books. Indeed, one of my friends described me as a compulsive writer. In 1985 I woke up one August night in the country with a very painful left shoulder. I returned home at once and an inner power compelled me to go to the hospital immediately. Here a dislocated head of the left humerus with a fracture of the lesser tuberosity was discovered on X-ray, and three weeks later an open operation was performed to reduce the dislocation and unite the fracture. The cause of this strange incident was correctly diagnosed as epilepsy, a common neurological condition which usually starts much earlier in life. None of my fits was of the classical major variety, and most were partial fits in which there was simply a transitory change in consciousness without any motor component. After some years I received the right medication, and I am now well stabilized.

My parish work continued well until the end of 1996 when my consciousness showed peculiar lapses and my walking, never very good, became more and more defective. I also developed a tremor of uncontrollable intensity; this was quite correctly diagnosed as Parkinson's disease, but it was unfortunately inadequately controlled medically. It certainly made my continuing parish work impracticable. About this time my right knee also became very painful, and two operations were performed on it. Nothing very significant was discovered, and my general health steadily deteriorated until the beginning of June 1997 when a major change in my consciousness occurred. I simply was not myself any more, and suffered from increasingly severe amnesia. There was an alarming state of confusion with strangely incoherent speech; indeed, I showed signs of a severe mental disturbance. At this stage various distressing physical signs also showed themselves. My carer Cliff returned from New Zealand on 7 June, by which time I was incontinent of urine, barely able to walk, and had very little strength. I was still able to communicate but only at a very basic level – simply 'Yes' and 'No' answers and much of what I said was irrelevant. This conversation on a rudimentary level was in startling contrast to the highly intelligent interplay that was my wont. Often all I could manage was a simple nod. I was totally unable to write or hold delicate objects.

Soon I became doubly incontinent, and was unable to swallow or walk. I could not hold myself up, and if I was placed in a chair, I simply slumped forward and needed to be supported to keep my head erect. It seemed as if I had suffered a complete systemic shutdown. The decline progressed with dramatic speed. I could not chew, so that any food given had to be pulped and liquidized. It appeared to my friends that I had totally given up, as if willing myself to die. I was during this whole phase in a semi-conscious state, which progressed to complete unconsciousness for more than six hours before I was finally admitted to hospital. Throughout this period I was in a state of total amnesia, but not entirely unconscious, because from time to time I could respond quite sensibly to comments. During this time I felt that I seemed to descend into a vast pit of darkness where I could 'sense' the souls of a vast concourse of people who were unknown to me personally. I seemed to be in hell, and even now I believe it might be possible that this was literally true. There was despair, darkness and a lack of communication between the souls that were there. The gloom was appalling, and there seemed to be no hope anywhere. In fact, I believe there was a total dissociation between my rational mind, which was shattered, and my spiritual mind which was forlorn and lonely but entirely free.

During this period many friends came to visit me, though I have no memory of this, and I received the Eucharist regularly from the Reserved Sacrament. I was also anointed on a number of occasions, and this might have been an important turning point in my recovery, for apparently I had lain in the balance between life and death for at least a week during the period of my complete amnesia.

The interesting thing about this entire period was a complete absence of fear, even though I was desolate and felt bereft of all human contact. Towards the end of this period I am told that I became quite communicative at times, especially with people I knew well, but I can remember nothing of this. I attained normal consciousness one morning in mid-July. It felt rather like waking up after a usual night's sleep, with the sunlight shining gloriously through the window, and I thought it was a Monday morning. It was the ward nurse who, with some amusement, told me that I had in fact been unconscious for five weeks. I was remarkably well oriented when I 'returned from the portals of death', but I still suffered from amnesia for recent events, and had completely lost the ability to walk. Even now, seven to eight months later, I am still largely confined to my wheelchair, but with the help of excellent physiotherapy and the constant support of my carer I am learning to walk with ever-increasing facility. I have often wondered whether my walking difficulty is not due to any disease of the nervous system, but is essentially the result of the total amnesia that afflicted me – in other words, I have forgotten how to walk, and have had to re-learn the process that I started when I was about one year old. For an elderly man this is no easy matter, to say the least!

Despite this terrifying experience I thank God for the privilege of experiencing it, because it has taught me so much and radically altered my personality and outlook on life.

I now know that we are all immortal, not through our own deserts, but by the immeasurably great love of God. I had long believed this on a mental level through my mystical nature, yet I could never entirely feel it in the depth of my soul. After I recovered normal consciousness, coming, as it were, back to myself once more, I knew that the supreme consciousness, which is one way of speaking of God, pervades all creation and loves it, whatever its nature and use may be. For us humans there is an individual as well as a collective destiny and the end is glorious, but this life is only one step towards that destiny, which no one alive can know with authority.

Incarnate life, because the body is frail, is bound to be involved in suffering, and its intensity bears no relationship to the character of the person. But the way of suffering is an essential part of the progress of the person towards self-knowledge and the recognition of God – the second follows the first (Luke 17:21). No one knows what will happen to them when they die, nor can they in their present state, though it is permissible to speculate. But as it was revealed to Julian of Norwich, all shall be well. The important duty in this life is that we should live as perfectly as we can in the present moment.

All this is a basic aspect of the spiritual life of all valid religious traditions, without the punitive aspect so often stressed by fundamentalists. Heaven cannot be attained until we are all in corporate unity, and this requires a change of heart in every person. There will therefore, after death, be a fresh openness to Divine reality.

My entire attitude to life has been changed by my 'return from the portals of death'. I am far less impatient with irritating people or disturbing circumstances than I was previously. I have now acquired a degree of acceptance which makes every moment not only tolerable, but even a joy in its own right. Another quite interesting change has been an acquisition of self-confidence, which was previously completely lacking in my character: I could not bear to hurt anybody's feelings and rejoiced in being well thought of by everybody. Indeed, my apparent virtue had far too much self-interest attached to it. Now I am much more clear-spoken than I was previously, and the cripplingly low self-esteem of the past has been replaced by confidence and trust. I can no longer expect to be liked by everybody nor even want it that way. It is much more important that I do my apportioned work as well as I can, irrespective of other people's opinions. This is incidentally quite a different attitude from that of irresponsible licence, which is so much a characteristic of our modern age. This explains why I do not spend time judging other people's way of life; it simply is not my business, for what I have to do with the relatively few years that still remain to me in this life is to be as helpful to others as I can, realizing that I am not special but merely a frail, fallible human being. This knowledge is the real focus of happiness as far as I am concerned. I do not look for any favours in the future, because they are always around us if only we had the self-control and the ability to be silent and appreciate them.

My period of convalescence was gradual. I immediately

recovered the memory of important names and events, but whole episodes of my life disappeared from my recall. Only as the months progressed did more and more of my memory return. Even now, it is a long way from being fully restored. In the early stages of my recovery I was very labile emotionally. When I discussed my experience with friends, particularly on the telephone but also to a lesser extent in direct conversation, I invariably broke down in describing the experience of descending into a vast pit of darkness where I could 'sense' the souls of people in a state of hell. It has taken quite a number of months for this emotional lability to disappear. When I was unconscious, I have been told, with some amusement, that I showed periods of great anger. I can well believe this, because in this state much emotional material that I had cautiously suppressed from public view had complete freedom of expression. It is interesting that even to this day I am much more outspoken than I was before the event and am much less concerned about people's opinions of me. Therefore, although I am possibly a 'nicer' person than before, I am certainly very much more of my own master. The freedom of living my own inner way that this has given me is remarkable.

I have no fear of death any more, so that even if I knew I were to die this very day, I would feel as detached as I would if I knew that up to thirty years' life lay ahead of me before the final event. I therefore am much less interested in such theories of the afterlife as heaven and hell, reincarnation or even the various promises made by different religions. What will be will be, and it is not my business to probe too deeply into matters beyond human understanding, at least in its present stage of development.

The last point concerns the diagnosis of this strange mental change that occurred when I was semi-conscious. I asked the consultant neurologist of the hospital where I was being treated what was really the matter with me, and he admitted that nobody knew for certain. One thing does appear, however, and that is when I was put on levodopa in adequate doses my condition changed quite noticeably.

When I entered hospital I was put on a life-support system for the first two days, after which I was sustained by intravenous therapy and finally by drinks containing essential nutrients. It is hardly surprising that I left hospital in an emaciated state.

Dr Oliver Sacks wrote a remarkable best-seller called *Awakenings*; it was first published in 1973 and has since then been through several editions and formats. The edition I have was published by Picador in 1990, and the book has since inspired a television documentary, radio and stage plays and a major feature film. It is obvious that it has attracted a far wider audience than merely the medical profession. In this remarkable, poignant book Dr Sacks described a number of cases that followed encephalitis lethargica, an epidemic of which occurred at the end of the First World War. Many patients died, but those that survived sometimes later entered a state of suspended animation which lasted up to forty years. They also showed various signs of complicated Parkinson's disease. The advent of levodopa in 1969 was hailed as one of the greatest medical discoveries of the century. When given orally to dormant patients they recovered full consciousness very rapidly as if it were a miracle; it became the great medical sensation for the next few years. But then, alas, while the original symptoms were greatly relieved, new manifestations showed themselves. These were not adverse drug reactions so much as other aspects of Parkinsonism. It was therefore obvious that the 'wonder drug' had its drawbacks as well as its advantages. Oliver Sacks' description of these patients before and after treatment is both dramatic and intensely moving. None of them was cured but the great majority showed variable degrees of improvement. All these patients have now died, and a great part of Sacks' book describes the tragic life that they had to bear in the wards of Mount Carmel Hospital in New York.

The type of Parkinsonism that I have had to cope with has been much simpler. The major symptoms were intense tremor and a tendency to rush forward when walking, but the question remains as to how much of the period of altered consciousness was Parkinsonian in origin. I questioned the neurologist specifically about this point, and he told me that my various symptoms could not be adequately explained in this way. But one thing is certain, since I have taken levodopa, there has been much less tremor and I am mentally up to scratch. Indeed, this book could not have been written were I not in that state of mental acuity.

The other question is, did I really have a near-death experience as I have claimed, or was the experience of dead people around me merely part of the disease? The usual near-death experience to which I alluded at the beginning of this chapter is very well recorded now and it is usually elevating; when people come 'down to earth' again they are resolved to lead a better life in future. But my experience was just the reverse of this; it indeed comes closer to a 'negative near-death experience'. In the *Sunday Telegraph* of 25 May 1997, page 3, reported by the Science Correspondent Robert Matthews, there was a description of patients who were desperately ill who saw visions of demons dragging them towards a pit, and they felt they had to fight desperately in order to keep alive.

A friend who visited me on several occasions when I was semi-conscious tends to dismiss all such experiences, whether positive or negative, as purely neurological phenomena, and there must be a considerable degree of truth in this argument, but Tony Lawrence, a lecturer in psychology at Coventry University, is much more agnostic about the matter. He tends to dismiss the suggestion of the images of heaven or hell as having a general cultural determining factor; people from many different cultures will describe meeting a figure of light (in the positive experience). They do not meet Jesus or Vishnu or Buddha, although afterwards they may sometimes describe what they saw in that way. Near-death experiences, whether positive or negative, cannot be attributed to the effects of medication or to the lack of oxygen reaching the brain in its final moments. Hallucinations brought on by drugs or anoxia are typically random and senseless. Another interesting fact is the reports of near-death experiences from hospital patients whose electro-encephalograph (EEG) traces become completely flat during resuscitation – showing that there was no activity in their brain.

To me, all this suggests that under certan circumstances, usually that of disease, but sometimes in apparently healthy people, the brain may be the recipient of anomalous information. Whether it is related to the physical state of the person or to some psychical or spiritual source remains to be discovered.

2 The illusion of wealth

If most people were asked what would really make them happy, they would say 'If only I had more money'. This would imply that their state of unease was due to a deficiency of material substance. There is no doubt that wealth brings in its wake an atmosphere of great security, and only a fool or a hypocrite would turn their nose up at it. Poverty cannot but produce unhappiness. On one level this denies the first of the monastic disciplines of poverty, chastity and obedience. Yet if one visits a religious community, particularly in our modern age, and in the more advanced European societies, one would neither expect nor find any evidence of great lack of material substance. Does this mean that the modern religious are failing in their basic calling, or indeed are frank hypocrites? The answer is most decidedly not – if indeed they were to follow this discipline to the letter, not only would their community suffer severely, but they also would fall victim to malnutrition, exposure to the elements and premature death. Therefore we can say at the beginning of this consideration that a total lack of concern with money is not the right way to happiness; on the contrary, such an attitude is bound to produce unhappiness as a consequence. This is not the end of the matter, because there is a type of poverty that leaves one free of personal responsibility, but in the end one cannot divorce oneself from the problems of other people and by extension of the whole world. The religious have sufficient means to be assured of survival and enough relaxation to achieve their allotted tasks well. So therefore poverty in itself is not a barrier to happiness provided one is doing one's work well and has no person to consider other than oneself. The essence of monastic poverty is in fact detachment from worldly things so that the mind may be concentrated on prayer.

> If thou shouldn'st never see my face again, pray for my soul.
> More things are wrought by prayer than this world dreams of.
> (Alfred, Lord Tennyson, *Idylls of the King*
> 'The Passing of Arthur', lines 407–8)

Only when one is totally in God can one begin to know happiness.

But what can we say about wealth itself, having demonstrated that poverty is seldom to be recommended? Surely a large amount of money should make one happy? Speaking from personal experience I can say emphatically that I know few millionaires whom I would describe as happy people. A surprising number have health problems while an insufficiency of work allows such problems the opportunity of taking over much of the plutocrat's attention. Nearly all of them have in fact acquired their wealth through inheritance, which is not the best way of becoming rich: in a way, their money has been thrust on them. They have acquired their riches through following a pre-determined path of education and life which, particularly in our present age, is usually a far from elevating one. The crux of the matter is this, that money is no guide to either the good life or its enjoyment. The former statement might conceivably be true to the average reader, but the latter is clearly paradoxical. What is there in wealth that usually prevents one enjoying it?

Apart from the obvious responsibility of taking care of it (and not infrequently of one's own life as well, in the face of robbers, kidnappers, and even murderers), there is the more basic element of devoting one's life to a selfish and ultimately unfulfilling way of acquisition of substance; while no one who knows themself properly would deny the importance of substance, when it becomes the ruling passion of one's life, it assumes a dictatorial power and even determines the types of people whom it is favourable to know on an intimate level. Therefore the cost of wealth may be a distortion of the normal pattern of one's life, even if that 'distortion' would be what many people would hanker after most happily. Money creates more money but it does not necessarily bring happiness with it. On the contrary, it adds responsibility and vulnerability and tends towards mixing predominantly with those who attain one's own social standing. It is very much a capitalist quality, and like all extreme capitalism it separates people into various strata of society. It is interesting at the moment that what was Communism in Eastern Europe has now been succeeded by a most grasping type of capitalism in which relatively few families possess most of the wealth of the country. Whether in the end this will bring with it greater freedom than existed under Communist tyranny will have to be seen; in my opinion, both are equally unsatisfactory forms of government, and the life that both produce becomes a personal prison. In Communism the walls of the prison are those of a particular ideology whereas in capitalism these walls are purely monetary. The one thing these conflicting ways of life have in common is their insubstantiality in as much as they both are liable to crumble at any time. Indeed, the recent collapse of European Communism is one of the marvels of our present age, though only a very naïve person could possibly rejoice at the present extreme capitalism which has now gripped some of these countries. The reason for this lack of present rejoicing is based on the divisive nature of capitalism, there being one law for the rich and another for the poor. All this goes to prove how very superficial the contentment based on wealth really shows itself when it is regarded as the *summum bonum* of the good life. It can certainly form part of its foundation, but one dwells very uneasily in its shadow.

I knew one man who did unexpectedly inherit a large amount of money and, from being a nobody, became a celebrity overnight. Not being in any way groomed for this change in fortune, he lived in a ridiculously extravagant way, as did his wife and family also. At last they could mix with the really important people around them! The thought of charity – giving rather than receiving, as St Paul would say, 'It is more blessed to give than to receive' (Acts 20:35) – came very slowly to this man; in fact, he began to see the real significance of wealth only when a great deal of his inheritance fell away from him through mismanagement and the dishonesty of some of his employees. In the darkness of his gloom (even then he was far richer than he had been before the legacy had come to him), he began to glimpse what wealth really meant and even more important why this sudden partial reversal of his fortune had to be experienced. Before then the idea of charity in the usual sense of giving money to deserving people and causes had never fully entered his head. This was not so much due to hard-heartedness as to a complete lack of awareness of how the rest of the world lived. It came to him with the same staggering illumination that struck St Paul on the road to Damascus when the risen Christ suddenly appeared to him. At once he began to investigate the whole question of charity and to find out what part he could play in relieving the want of those less fortunate than he was. He actually started to give money in his relatively impoverished state, and at once an enormous load fell from him; at last he could become aware of something else rather than his own disappointment. He gave to and patronized deserving causes, and as happens so frequently, his own investments such as were still available began to grow in wealth. Within about ten years he had recovered his loss completely, but then he was much more detached from his own misfortune and equally much more attached to the misfortunes of other people. His marriage, which was beginning to founder on the rocks of infidelity, weathered the storm, and he began to appreciate the individual beauty of his previously neglected wife, who before then had been more of a showpiece than a companion. In the end, he attained national prominence with a title, but he had now gained sufficient independence from the opinions of other people that he could order his own life according to what his growing conscience told him.

'It is easier for a camel to pass through the eye of a needle than for a rich man to enter the kingdom of God' (Matthew 19:24).

Wealth that could lead to happiness

It is evident from what has already been said that there is an intrinsic ambivalence in wealth – in itself it neither leads to happiness nor does its deficiency invariably result in unhappiness, even if the tendency is obvious. What, then, can lead to happiness in the life that is blessed with riches? I would think that the really important factor is how the riches have been acquired. Inherited wealth, as we have already said, tends if anything to a subtle type of incarceration. On the other hand, if the wealth has accrued from a very modest base, it could be the basis of a satisfying life.

Consider, for instance, the case of a person who was born in decidedly poor circumstances and when they had attained adult life had to work extremely hard to make ends meet. Through great effort they were able to acquire secondary education, perhaps a university degree, and some sort of career was then open to them. It might, for instance, have been setting up a small business or else entering the professional field of medicine, law or accountancy. By dint of hard work and relatively honest endeavour (no life other than that of Christ could possibly be perfect on a moral level), this person could maintain their position in the society in which they lived; they may have married and had children and as the years rolled by and their family grew up, their savings might have accrued from a modest income. It would never have been particularly great in the early years for obvious reasons, and indeed much of this might well have been a severe material struggle. But in the end, as later middle age drew near, and the family attained its own maturity, they could relax and to their amazement they might find that they were quite well off. This, of course, apart from rare instances of innovative genius, would be the result of intelligent investment of capital allied to a sensible style of living. The money had been laid by primarily for emergencies but later with retirement it was available for relaxation and travel as well.

If one were naïve, one might believe that the happiness was confined to the latter part of this hypothetical person's life, but I dare say that when the end was drawing near that same person would begin to acknowledge that their whole adult life had had its own satisfaction; they were as happy as struggling young people as they were when financially independent at the latter part of their existence. If one considers this case even more deeply, it is evident how secondary the financial aspect really proved in the happiness of the family; it certainly was an important foundation of the happiness but it did not really contribute very much to its overall fulfilment.

This small example illustrates two aspects of wealth in relation to happiness: its use in relieving want and its radiance when it is used for the benefit of other people and charitable work in general. As soon as it emerges in triumph, either through insecurity or pride, it becomes ugly and grasping. If it does no other harm, it tends to exalt the rich person above their true station in the community, and when it departs at the moment of death, the soul (assuming that there is survival of death in this way) can have nothing of it. What it has gained is the life experience of the individual when they were incarnate, and those who are wise recognize that this is the supreme value of all human life; all possessions are by their very nature transient, either perishing with time or else being bequeathed to those who follow on when the person dies. Such is the way of life; it combines with it elements of tragedy and comedy, the latter being most grotesque when the individual lays particularly great stress upon material possessions.

It seems that the value of the things on this earth, which I have included under the conception of substance, is that they teach us both responsibility and the transient nature of the very things that we value most. This does not mean for one moment that worldly affairs are trivial, but it does show that their importance is of limited duration. Our lives have two important ends in view, personal growth and caring for others, who include not only human beings but all life in the world which we inhabit; if we are stupid enough to appropriate even a molecule of this for our own possession, we will soon find that it has disappeared from our grasp, and this is as it should be; St Paul puts it thus: 'For the earth is the Lord's and all that is in it' (1 Corinthians 10:26). He alone has control of the universe in its vastness and also in its minuteness, and we are mere ciphers in a tremendous interplay of cosmic life. We are at our most important when we are silent and do the work appropriate for us in quietness and efficiency. These qualities do not mix well with possessiveness and pride.

It is a fundamental rule of life that comparisons are odious; even the poisonous snake and the spider have uses in the creative order which even the most brilliant human mind might not fathom. When one knows this, far from feeling inferior or at any rate a failure, an immense burden of assumed responsibility drops from one, and one can participate more joyfully with all creation in the present moment. This fact interestingly enough has little to do with wealth; indeed, the poor who have never expected very much for themselves are nearer this state of 'self-abandonment to Divine providence' (the title of a spiritual classic by Jean-Pierre de Caussade) than the wealthy. The latter are frequently so much immersed in their own possessions that they have little time to see beyond them. It must be very daunting to own a great deal (something few of us are liable to experience in our life), for one's attention is inevitably fixed on one's possessions while the glorious flow of life itself often passes before our gaze unacknowledged. It is this that makes me particularly sceptical about the overall desirability of great wealth. Once it gets in the way of living in the present, it becomes increasingly burdensome until one's whole life is bound up with its maintenance.

Another interesting observation about affluence is that often the more one has, the less meaning it has for one. This applies particularly to the children of rich parents. While some may conceivably inherit the drive of their parents, many more will tend to loiter in its results. They may well enter a drug culture or occasionally even set up a business based on a non-existent foundation. In the lifestyle of our present age it would often appear that basic moral values are sedulously ignored, and the perceived pleasure of the moment is the only thing that gives satisfaction. An increasing number of children who hail from rich, distinguished families end up in disgrace, whether moral or financial. As the well-known saying has it, 'The devil always has work in plenty for idle hands to do'. If our minds are not concentrated on constructive activities, they will soon wander off through trivialities to indecency, crime and destructiveness. Our century has shown this in no uncertain way.

A fundamental aspect of money is that it is usually a spur to useful activity, but until society moves beyond assessing people's worth according to their means, there will be unhappiness in the world and a general discontent. I have in my own experience known that I am at my happiest when I am doing work without payment. I am thinking here particularly of such activities as exorcism, healing and counselling. When I started this work, some 35 years ago, I made a vow at its inception never to charge anybody anything for my services. This obviously took up a considerable amount of my time, for it was my intention not to cut short any period of interview under an hour. In the end I became very ill, but I cannot in all truth equate my recent illness with the previous work I had been doing, and in any case I would have done it again with much greater illness than I have had to bear. To me the greatest happiness has always lain in bringing happiness to other people. On its own such a statement could well apply to Job before his terrible smash, but in fact it was not so in my case; I did this because of the great sympathy I had for many others like myself, who suffered from abysmally low self-esteem. I knew very well that many people had a completely different view of my abilities, but I was only too aware of the insignificance of these plaudits.

The greatest joy that I have known is to have been able to play even a small part in the restoration of someone else from the darkness of suffering to the light of full life. When I started this work I did not know what I was doing; at a certain point in my life I was introduced to the healing ministry, which in turn entailed priesthood and serving others in a way that I have previously described. This has been the crowning satisfaction of my life and, if anything, I have been confused when people have spoken well of me, because in my heart of hearts I am still amazed, almost to the point of incredulity. Had it been otherwise, I could never have done any good work at all, for I would always have been comparing myself with others in the same field of endeavour. In addition, there would have been an exciting financial incentive. I thank God that these two not inconsiderable temptations were denied me at the very beginning, and now as an elderly man I can at least look back on this period of my life with neither regret nor shame.

Yet, while I was living in a natural austerity, comparable in its way to that of someone in monastic orders, my basic capital increased through sound investment. Now crippled, at least temporarily, by an obscure illness that I have already described, I can afford carers and a life-style which is quite adequate to my needs. As one gets older it is obvious that one's needs increase; that is why it is not inappropriate that death should dominate this stage in a person's life. But the wealth that really matters is the experience of life that one has attained during its flow. The fruits of that work are the happiness that other people have attained through it and the growth that one has manifested unknown to oneself at the same time. This is in fact the real wages of work done without price to other people.

I have to say through experience, however, that one cannot even begin to do this sort of work until one is inwardly strong, for otherwise people would quite involuntarily and unconsciously lean on one. This is undesirable for two reasons; first, one is drained of one's own inner resources, and second, the other person, in their leaning, fails to grow strong in their own experience. This, of course, is seen physiologically and psychologically in the lives of all of us during the period of childhood and less so in adolescence. The last thing anyone involved in this work should look for is acknowledgement; the work of Jesus and his attitude to it are crowning examples. Otherwise one would end in a state of angry disillusionment with the whole world!

When everyone in our world has achieved the patience and dedication to follow this way of life, we will all be on the way to becoming full human beings, even sanctification, if one thinks in those terms. Our lives, though individually private, cease to be cut off from the main flow of people, but are instead shared with many others in our common journey to fulfilment as children of God. At that point there will be no need of saints but rather ordinary people who do their allotted task well and with consideration and joy for the world at large. Money attains its greatest contribution for good when it ceases to be a private possession and becomes a universal gift. Then it is a true blessing for the whole world.

3 The place of power

How can one attain power without being a menace to other people? The first requirement is a deepening self-knowledge. When one knows one's own character, at least to some extent, one can begin to curb its excesses and even start to listen to other people rather than always dictate to them. But how does one listen to other people? If one were really honest about this, one seldom listens attentively until one recognizes one's own ignorance, then one can at least begin to learn. As one gains self-knowledge in this way, so one can enter more adequately into the lives of other people. This 'empathy' is the first stage of power being shared with others, and mitigates its corrupting influence. The more one is in harmony with others, the more one sympathizes with their particular problems. There is fortunately in the depth of most of us a tendency to help (in addition to the more forcible proclivity to selfishness and acquiring everything for ourself). The more avidly we can empathize in a mutual way, the more the inner spark of love that burns in all of us begins to ignite into a flame, and then power ceases to be so much a corrupting influence as one which aims at helping other people in a non-attached way. I use the expression 'non-attached' deliberately; it differs from mere detachment in that, while leaving the other person free, it does what it can to help, whereas pure detachment leaves the person alone and gets on with its own business.

One always has to be aware of the attraction of helping other people while there also burns inside a tendency to dominate them. How easy, and at the same time how enjoyable it is to insinuate oneself into other people's affairs! These are none of one's own business, but they do afford a diversion, interesting oneself in matters that help take one's mind off personal problems. The 'Lady Bountiful' that lies in the hearts of many 'do-gooders' gains its satisfaction by interfering, and at the same time, feeling radiant in the process of delivering others from difficulties and distress. If one is really unaware of one's own weakness, the satisfaction of this procedure is especially attractive when others speak well of one. If one has very little self-knowledge, one can easily relax in the warmth of other people's praise, only to discover in the end that one is becoming more increasingly a general nuisance. What should be a chorus of gratitude becomes a litany of rejection. I personally am always wary of people who donate large amounts of money to charities, because I, no doubt of a sceptical frame of mind, can so easily see the self-satisfaction that lies at the root of much charitable action. Does this, therefore, mean that I have no place for giving money in my life? I sincerely hope not, but I feel that the most valuable giving is of the whole person. One should give in such a way that the left hand does not know what the right hand bequeaths. As Jesus says: 'Beware, when people speak well of you, for so they did also of the false prophets who preceded you' (Luke 6:26).

A great attraction of worldly power is its tendency to exalt the social position of the person who wields it. At one time this type of power was closely related to the wealth of the individual, but at present the remarkable reversal of so many social roles has made poverty also a focus of power. I speak here quite deliberately of political parties that emphasize their left-wing stance; this in itself is rather to be encouraged, for it is disgraceful that the poor should continue to be marginalized as they have been since time immemorial. No one who has visited a country such as India can be other than revolted at the stark poverty that confronts them even as they leave their luxurious hotel. The real criticism of the tendency to overcome at least some of the more flagrant abuses of wealth is that it has been accompanied by a language of rights. This again on its own is quite in order, but when rights begin to become important as a political issue it is necessary for them to be counterbalanced by the concept of responsibilities. The concept of the welfare state is a splendid ideal, but we need to remember the bears of North America, which expect handouts rather than having to seek their own survival in a harsh environment. The immediate benefits are obvious, but just as people cannot live on bread alone, but only on every word that comes from the mouth of the Lord (Deuteronomy 8:3), so material benefits are an indifferent means of sustenance until the person's inner constitution can cope with all the qualities of the life they are obliged to lead. On the other hand, there are many people in desperate straits who require immediate assistance – it is for such as these that a welfare state is an essential lifeline.

Power can be the attraction that leads to social eminence and personal corruption, or else it may be the way forward to a stronger, healthier person, more able to serve their community. Once again, this demonstrates the very ambivalent nature of power, but being what most of us are, we prefer the softer option. The end of this type of power, based on eminence and social position, cannot do other than lead to social conflict which will in due course culminate in enmity, rivalry and war. This, indeed, is the terrible consequence of power that is improperly used.

Closely allied to the social position engendered by power is personal status in the eyes of the world. This too is one of the products of wealth, stressing the close relationship of wealth to power; the emotional link is that of ambition, which may be defined as the ardent desire for distinction. This does not always have to be related to power on a social level; it can quite as easily be the end result of brilliance in the fields of the arts, the sciences and philosophy with its numerous variations. Quoting the words of Edward George Bulwer-Lytton,

Beneath the rule of men entirely great,
The pen is mightier than the sword.
                                    (*Richelieu*, II.ii)

This indicates that the power of the mind is the really dominating agent of important actions.

It was not merely the force behind the emancipation of slaves, but also the inspiration of numerous terrible actions in the realms of religion and politics. The most outstanding example in the twentieth century was the power that elevated an unknown man, Adolf Hitler, into one of the most appalling and destructive dictators in the history of the human race. The power wielded by Hitler was the ultimate basis of terrible genocide, which could not conceivably be repaired by the good deeds of many philanthropists. But if one were to leave the subject on that note, something vital would be missing: none of us is worth much on their own, but a really noble thought can inspire the lives of millions and set them on the right path. This is, in my opinion, the supreme achievement as well as vital necessity of greatness in the realms of art. What on the surface could be more frail than music, painting or literature? But when it strikes the right note, it can change the lives of many people. One can indeed understand the might of the pen in this way and the supreme responsibility that those with the gift of communication have in directing the uncivilized thoughts of so many 'average people' from sheer self-satisfaction to aspiration on behalf of many others.

This, I believe, can be the only effective way to a real transformation of society from the unstable conflict of our present world into something at least vaguely reminiscent of the Utopia which all politicians canvass at the time of their election, but few, if any, are capable of producing when they have their brief term of office at the helm of power. Speeches, in other words, may be extremely convincing, but their promise is often short-lived; great thoughts, on the other hand, may remain in a smouldering phase for some time, but when they do ignite, an enormous conflagration may be the result, a result perhaps significant enough to change the course of history. In my opinion, the study of history finds its end in demonstrating the course of human nature over many centuries, and I am optimistic enough to believe with Julian of Norwich that all will be well in the end, even if I have to add the rider that the going can be pretty hard at times.

In the rather forbidding Parable of the Talents we read the dictum: 'For everyone who has will be given more, till he has enough and to spare; and everyone who has nothing will forfeit even what he has' (Matthew 25:29). This statement applies to those who bury their innate gifts instead of sharing them with the whole community. This is, in fact, even more true of the ultimate end of the dictators of history – they emerge as flashes of lightning and after their brief, usually highly destructive, reign are summarily extinguished, whereas those who are beneficent and constructive burn steadfastly on until their time of recognition comes, when they influence an increasing number of people and are seen as the true heroes of the human race. Without their power they could have done nothing of value, and had that power been self-directed it would have emerged evil and distorted.

The truth is quite obvious; what we have is not our own property, but at the most we are guardians of it. We are admittedly not expected to give everything away and to starve, but our great work is to preserve our gifts and increase their scope, so that they may be left in an enriched state when we have departed this life for our own unknown future. In fact, if one has lived constructively, one's own end becomes increasingly unimportant to one, and it is the future of the whole human race that arrests our attention. No wonder many of the world's great religions, particularly those of the East, stress the importance of non-attachment to worldly things.

Power reaches its apogee when it gives of itself freely and lovingly to those around. Then it ceases to demonstrate its own strength, but instead rejoices in being able to identify with all those around it. If I, for instance, pride myself on some particular gift that I might have, I will simply take refuge from my true being in some peripheral quality that I may possess. This quality is bound to be challenged and superseded by those who come after me, and here I allude especially to the ageing process, which is a threat to the egoist, but a source of increasing relief to the person who has lived intelligently and given up their life for the concern of the whole community. It is indeed a wonderful thing to see an individual with power used rightly, for then so much good can come out of it. It ceases to be a means of protection of the self but rather expands to take under its wing all other people and, indeed, all life itself.

In our very warped world, one of the features of encouragement is what might be called the ecological revolution – that we are no longer creatures solely involved in our own survival, but it is our responsibility to embrace life in general. Then the brotherhood of all creation may be more than merely an elevating concept but a very urgent fact of life. The words of Jesus come to mind: 'Come to me, all who are weary and whose load is heavy; I will give you rest. Take my yoke upon you, and learn from me, for I am gentle and humble hearted; and you will find rest for your souls. For my yoke is easy to wear, my load is light' (Matthew 11:28–9). The power of Jesus is recognized not so much by the miracles he performed or his courageous stance in the presence of the hypocritical religious leaders that challenged him, but even more so by his unafraid attitude that led to Gethsemane and the journey to Calvary. What impresses me particularly was his complete lack of resistance of any type. Jesus's final statement was 'Father, forgive them; they do not know what they are doing' (Luke 23:34).

These thoughts occur again in the life of St Paul in his second letter to the Corinthians; after describing wonderful mystical experiences, he is brought sharply down to earth again by a mysterious illness which he calls a thorn in the flesh from Satan sent to buffet him. He begged three times to God to rid him of this malady, but the answer was 'My grace is all you need; power is most fully seen in weakness'. He was therefore happy to boast of his weakness, because then the power of Christ would rest upon him. So he was content with a life of weakness, insult, hardship, persecution and distress, all for Christ's sake. He finishes with the crucial deduction, 'For when I am weak, then I am strong' (2 Corinthians 12:7–10).

This is the culmination of power well used, and it does not develop overnight. It follows the slow grind of life, full of disappointments and betrayal as well as personal triumph and happiness. The proper course of power is paradoxically enough its failure in terms of the expectations common to us all, and its end is not victory but submission, to which forgiveness is added. The person who can forget what they were in the world's eyes and how powerful at the height of their ascendancy is also the one whose life has been a blessing. This was undoubtedly the way of Christ, but we lesser beings need not be completely abashed by its nobility; each of our lives has its own tragedy, and to be able to surmount this is the real victory of life over death. I have always suspected that we all have our own individual destiny to fulfil, and it seldom becomes easier as it moves towards its end. But, if we persist with unfailing trust, we will not end disappointed.

In a very paradoxical way, happiness comes to us when we have disposed freely of our possessions, the greatest of which is our own personality. When we have made ourselves fully available to our neighbour and to God, becoming nothing in the process, then at last we begin to live. This is stated thus in the form of Jesus' paradox: 'Whoever gains his life will lose it; whoever loses his life for my sake will gain it' (Matthew 10:39). This applies, of course, primarily to Jesus, but his life as the life of God, is projected into all our lives so therefore we should always love our neighbour as ourself. This is the second of Jesus' two great commandments.

Knowing oneself

Self-knowledge is a life-long process. It starts on a starkly egoistical basis during early childhood, but soon we have to learn that other people around us not only have their own concerns but also react to us in their own particular fashion. In this way we are steadily nurtured from a selfish view that we are the centre of the universe to the infinitely more realistic understanding that we are merely tiny portions of an ever-expanding world which is destined to continue long after we have passed away. Yet in the very fact of our frailty and the evanescence of life itself lies our own unique contribution – not in strength but so much more in our mortal weakness. Not infrequently when we appear at our most trivial, our significance stands out to those near us, because then, at that very moment, we can fully and spontaneously empathize with the other person.

This is also our moment of full self-knowledge, which is something quite apart from the *persona* we present, or would like to present, to the world. To know oneself as a genuine person entails the casting off of superficial masks that we enjoy exhibiting, such as intellectual ability, social eminence, artistic skill or our physical appearance, and instead revealing ourselves naked to the world. It means discarding all social distinctions and political prejudices, so that we can face whatever circumstance may confront us directly and without embarrassment. Then the quality of one's antecedents or even one's own past history, whether creditable or disgusting, ceases to matter.

This is how we may glimpse something of the love of God, that we are treasured for what we are, and that the special use we make of this is of only secondary importance. This is what it means to know oneself truly. Once this has been given to one, all previous short-comings are simply things of the past. One's repentance has in fact been effected by one's previous openness to the truth of one's own character. This has been the vital purge preceding the essential self-knowledge that alone can make power a safe possession. When one no longer desires it, it never leaves one and furthermore it pours out gratuitously to all and sundry who may come to one for help day by day.

4 Health in relationship to happiness

If there is one quality that would appear obviously to determine a person's happiness, that quality would be health. We normally take health for granted until we injure ourselves or fall victim to some illness; only then do we value the joy of having a healthy body. When we are well, on the other hand, far from being grateful for this, we are much more likely to grumble about other matters that are disturbing us.

As we get older, we are all bound to come to terms with the failure of our bodies. None of us is exempt from the slow decay that is part of the mortal frame. The interesting thing about age generally is how what was once almost intolerable to consider is gradually approached without our thinking about it at all. A young person of, say, 20 years would have regarded a 60- or 70-year-old man or woman as very old indeed, but nowadays with the remarkable increase in longevity common in humans generally, these ages are the rule rather than the exception. Most people when they reach the 'age of retirement' (usually about 65 years) feel that, provided they have saved enough money, they are entitled to spend the remaining portion of their life in relaxation. This may involve travel, reading, or entertainments of one type or another; in the end, a failure of one of the senses or of the mental faculty tends to narrow the possibilities, at least as far as personal actualization is concerned. But fortunately, there are other elderly people with active minds who can really start to live properly when the grind of daily work has at last been surmounted by an adequate pension. They may either follow the desire of their mind, or else branch out into some new activity. Age is certainly not the insuperable barrier that it was in times past, and elderly people can now achieve much involving the mind and body which would have seemed well nigh impossible before.

No one but a fool could deny the vital part that good health plays as a basis for happiness, whether personal or communal, but is the reverse equally true? Do people suffering from chronic ill-health of one type or another always have to be miserable? It all depends on what that person makes of their fate. The usual response will be to take refuge behind ill-health from fulfilling one's daily responsibilities, and no one who has suffered can fail to sympathize with this attitude. But what about the person who can triumph over ill-health, as we have seen St Paul do? But even his predicament is not the abyss of ill-health; it was more likely an inconvenience that interfered with his unique ministry. To me, the supreme example of a person triumphing over a condition that was never going to get better but, on the other hand, got progressively worse with the years, was Beethoven afflicted by his deafness.

The first signs of this ailment became apparent when he was still young in his musical profession, and he tried various ways of coping with it. Nowadays those who are deaf can be helped by electrical amplifiers that can make clearer what little hearing they still possess, but in his day nothing much could be done. Nevertheless, after a brief period of extreme depression he fought back and all his greatest music was written under the shadow of progressively increasing deafness, which reached its culmination before his composition of the five last quartets. He communicated by writing since he could hear nothing other people said to him. This handicap would have been terrible enough for any of us, but one can hardly imagine how appalling it must have been for a composer not to have been able to hear his own music. Indeed, the ways of genius are chastening as well as inspiring, and his heroism is beyond praise.

Many others who do not have great gifts of creativity also

labour under failing hearing or sight. They can either retire into inner darkness or they can enjoy the world for what it is, despite their terrible handicap. Are these people simply to be pitied? The answer relies entirely on their own response; they can either see it as a terrible blow of fate and wither accordingly under its blast, or they can respond creatively. This to me is the power of Beethoven's music, which has a uniquely heroic quality that has stirred many people in times of great darkness.

Modern medicine now takes better care of us than before, but we all have to bear the fact of ultimate death. The end of all life is death; what matters is what one has made of one's life and what sort of death one may reasonably expect. Let it be said at once that no one alive in the flesh can know what happens when they die, or even what it feels like to die. With certain rare exceptions the 'near-death experience' is fleeting and rather attractive. To the very few that have had a very profound glimpse of death (as I believe I was given), there is a darker element also. This I think is probably the proper sequence of events that follow any life lived to its full adult stature. It could not apply in the same way to young children who die prematurely.

The more one considers the whole matter of survival, the more one is confronted with unanswerable questions. I do not believe that we are equipped to penetrate these matters with our present range of understanding. What, I believe, we are expected to do, is to live our lives as perfectly as we can at the present moment. Jesus puts it thus in the Sermon on the Mount: 'Set your mind on God's kingdom and his justice before everything else, and all the rest will come to you as well. So do not be anxious about tomorrow; tomorrow will look after itself. Each day has troubles enough of its own' (Matthew 6:33–4).

Health is never a purely personal matter, because it involves the entire society in which we live. Only when people generally are satisfied with their living conditions can the corporate society be healthy. Here, of course, we come up against the problems of socialism and capitalism; the first would tend to even things out so that everyone lived at a modest level, but little reward would come to those with special gifts or talents, while the latter would produce a marginalized society with only the favoured few at the centre of the stage. Neither of these is healthy. But the question then comes to mind, is any type of social health compatible with the human condition? To my way of thinking, the healthy society can only evolve when people themselves are changed from merely grasping animals to souls who are prepared to sacrifice themselves for the benefit of others. Self-sacrifice, as we have already said, seems to be a prerequisite for happiness, for when we are nothing, then at last we can forget ourselves – including ill health of various types – and give of ourselves fully to the people around us. It is quite easy to prescribe remedies for various obvious social evils and injustices with the full inner knowledge that these solutions have little practical reality and are merely ways of demonstrating our own goodwill. It is only when we have hit the bottom and have miraculously risen up again that we can identify ourselves fully with various social ills that previously we would never have known face to face. When this happens, we are actually forced to broaden our concern to embrace the masses of society who live at subsistence level, and then we can begin to play our part in healing the many rifts in the society of which we are a part.

When we see health in this very much larger context than merely the personal view, we are focusing on the great mystery of life itself. Health is the foundation stone of personal and communal life and on this foundation the quest for happiness can begin. Yet there is a deeper quest than even health, and that is our inner creativity; great works of art are known to have emerged in the minds of geniuses when their material circumstances could hardly have been more degrading. I often wonder whether Beethoven might have been, if anything, a more prosaic composer had he been able to hear perfectly. His handicap became a great challenge to an equally great soul. People of that stature do not attempt to opt out of the race for life itself; on the contrary, their lust for life is sharpened by their handicap. I often think with grief of Mozart, Schubert, Keats, Van Gogh and many other geniuses in the arts who died at lamentably early ages, and then a wiser mentor from the depth of my own being comes to me and tells me that it had to be. It would appear that they had completed their destiny in this particular life and it was time for them to move on to that unknown future that confronts us all when our lives are over. Hence, as I have already said, live perfectly in the moment, for we do not know what even the next moment will bring, either in terms of success or failure. What appears to be a failure, as occurs so often in the realm of the arts, is recognized many years later (quite often long after the genius has died) as an immortal achievement. I myself find the music of the eighteenth and nineteenth centuries of the greatest inspiration, whereas most contemporary music leaves little impact on me. This does not mean, needless to say, that this music is necessarily inferior to what preceded it, but that I am merely a typical child of my own time.

When one can drive oneself against the odds and persist in one's efforts, as when the body would much prefer to be in the state of permanent relaxation, then can greatness show itself in all of us. There is obviously a time when we have to yield to the demands of the body, but also a time in the course of a chronic disease when one should react positively against it. It is in this fight for survival that even the least brave of people can show their heroism. It is no doubt much easier to be a hero on the battlefield than to contend valiantly against the failure of vital functions in one's own body. The great person need not necessarily be a spectacular achiever of creative wonders; their glory consists in being true to themselves when the whole world seems to be falling about around them.

The attainment of health

How does one know that one is healthy or at least on the path towards the attainment of health? The mind seems to play a crucial part in this understanding. There is a sense of purpose in one's life which reveals a key towards its fulfilment. A healthy body is the outer reflection of a mind filled with satisfying images. If these images were entirely material; their futility would soon become obvious. We have already considered some of these images in the form of wealth and power. These are as likely to take one's mind off the main theme of living as to promote its onward flow. When one knows intuitively that one is on the right path, the body expands correspondingly. Thus the company one keeps and the work one is doing, if satisfactory and constructive, show themselves externally in the form of health.

Health, of course, is not merely a matter of external circumstances. We are constantly assailed by noxious agents as well as the hostility of various social pressures. These are not to be merely regarded as intruders in our private environment, but as ever-assailing forces that prevent us getting stuck in our present self-satisfaction. We slowly begin to understand that health is far more than merely a state of bodily contentment but one of infinite progress towards the barely discernible ideal of heaven on earth. This, as already indicated, is never a primarily individual state, because it has profoundly important social implications. As John Donne put it so memorably, 'No man is an *Island* entire of its self. Any man's *death* diminishes *me*, because I am involved in *Mankind*; And therefore never send to know for whom the *bell* tolls; it tolls for *thee*' (*Devotions upon Emergent Occasions*).

In all our lives the state of our body affects our basic outlook; anatomy is indeed destiny, as I believe Freud once said. We have thought about this already in relationship to Beethoven's deafness. It is interesting that the state of health of nations on a primarily physical level is now appreciated by all Western countries, and increasingly so by those of the East also, and this is as it should be. One cannot build a happy society when its members are collectively fighting battles of daily survival. And yet, paradoxically, it is the surmounting of these constant encounters that not only ensures the continuance of the species but also its upward, spiritual growth. If there were no struggles for survival, we would all soon lapse into a comfortable type of desiccating uniformity, but there is something deep inside us all that will not let us be until we have completed the work that we have been scheduled to do. It is a divine discontent. We alone are able to know the nature of that work, but until it is under way we are not in a genuine state of health. This is the real reason why such attractions as wealth and power may afford are in the end very superficial indeed.

But what about the type of person, apparently very common indeed, who can see no purpose in life other than acquiring as much as possible for themselves (and their families also)? It is no use preaching to these people – if indeed preaching is of any value at all, except to those who are already on the way to conversion to a nobler form of life than that commonly canvassed. Such people have to learn the inadequacy of their limited, self-centred way of existence by its results in such terms as ill-health, financial disaster and family breakdown. The great question in most people's lives is 'Why did it have to happen to me?' The answer is actually extremely simple: 'It had to be so because there were numerous lessons that you had still to learn in order to be healthy as an entire person.' Even Job, though a perfectly righteous man, had to learn that doing all the good in the world was inadequate as long as he derived satisfaction from placing himself in his own mind above the position of those whom he helped. There is indeed no justice in our life so long as we expect it in terms of personal approbation. We can only begin to approach the portals of happiness when we have merged with our fellow creatures, which is another way of saying when we have surrendered our ego in the greater flow of life itself. I have come to see ill health in this much greater context of existence through participating in life in a state of pain; when one knows one is not special, then at last one is entering the healthy life. In the usual way of paradox, when we know we are nothing we are beginning our unique contribution in the world at large.

This understanding of health places such medical factors as heredity, infection and the degenerative processes consequent on ageing in their proper perspective. They are simply the inevitable way in which any living organism matures and ages, and none of us can be immune from their inroads. Real health, however, sees this as merely the springboard of the development of the soul, or true nature of the individual, which is not destined to destruction when the body dies, but, on the other hand, only begins to experience a far freer health when it is no longer tied to the ageing process native to all material things. The end of life is obviously death, but the end of death, though still rationally obscure, is spiritually illuminated by an understanding of the immortality of life which can be glimpsed only as a result of Divine inspiration.

5 Friendship:
a key to happiness

When we are young most of us have a very superficial, yet embracing concept of friendship. Our school contemporaries tend to be regarded *en masse* as friends provided we have a mutual respect and liking one for another. Friendship assumes a deeper part of our life when we are in personal difficulty and need to rely on the support of our friends for our deliverance. This at once diminishes the number of friends who are reliable and true to us. In other words, when life is easy we are surrounded by a large group of well-wishers, but when the journey is more rugged most of them simply drop off. They appear to have more important things to do with their lives than come to our assistance. It is at this time that we realize how equally superficial our relation-ships are with many whom we call our friends. Therefore the essential quality of a true friendship is its capacity to support the friend even to our own disadvantage.

This disadvantage may simply involve setting aside time to be with our friend, but sometimes it may also require lending money or giving our support by acts of self-denial on behalf of the person in difficulty. All this is excellent but if it is to be real and not merely an illusory passion, the relationship must assume permanence. Therefore a friend-ship has as its emotional basis a warm affection for another person to whom we feel an attachment, liking or fondness. There seems to be something in the 'emotional chemistry' of two people that draws them together; this need not have anything to do with their political affiliation or even sex; it is by no means impossible for a man and a woman to have this platonic friendship, which has no erotic quality at all. Personally, I do not believe that any relationship is entirely free of a sexual character, but it is only when there is a strongly physical element attached to it that it moves beyond intimate friendship to conjugal love. This is obviously closely related to friendship and yet poles apart from it at the same time. This is the interesting part of human personality, that people may be drawn together physically while remaining cold on a deeper emotional level. The three evangelical virtues of faith, hope and love often do not recognize this harsher desiring aspect of love, and so the word is often degraded, but if it retains its charitable nature it does indeed form the climax of the three virtues.

Friends are joined together in intimacy and mutual benevolence independently of sexual or family love, but of course the real family ought to be a group of intimate friends. Anyone who has dealt with family problems, which seem to be the rule rather than the exception nowadays, knows that the family may be a little monster as easily as a group of loving friends. It is, in my opinion, for this reason that family life is so important in the development of the great majority of people, and its end is usually, though by no means always, reproduction. As one who is a natural celibate, I have the advantage of viewing the whole scene with a detached benevolence through which I can see so many aspects of a disturbed family relationship. When people start to disagree violently with each other it is evident that their friendship is still at only an early stage of development. I am not implying by this that real friends never have disagreements, but simply that enduring friendships do not materialize overnight. If our friends had to agree with us on every point at issue, we would be surrounded only by sycophants. The value of any true relationship, whether in marriage or apart from marriage, is that we grow through inevitable disagreement to a deeper awareness of the person we really are with the support of those who may disagree quite strongly with us on matters that, if we saw things properly, would turn out to be trivial idiosyncracies. In my own life there are some people who laud me to the skies whom I have learnt to regard with low esteem – whereas others who do not mind cutting me down to my true size remain my valued friends. Self-esteem comes as a result of doing one's work as well as one can and also being as concerned about others as is possible. It should not be the result of the opinions of other people, even if these opinions are completely justified. A true friend will never leave one in the lurch, while at the same time having their own particular life to lead, which is quite independent of one's own. A friend who disappoints one by failing to lend a helping hand during a time of adversity is clearly not a friend at all, and in this discovery, if one is wise, one should begin to see the inadequacy of one's own friendship also. In this life, it is a general rule that we get what we deserve, though the going may be very hard, and if we try to find scapegoats for our own unhappiness, we should start by looking very closely within ourselves.

I often wonder how many friends Jesus had. There were few, if any, in high places, and even the twelve apostles showed their painful weakness when they could have been of most assistance to him. The role of Judas Iscariot has never ceased to fascinate me; he is the obvious villain of the story, but without his rather obscure betrayal and the result of it, the Christian religion, as we know it, would never have emerged. These are thoughts that do not fit in well with comfortable orthodoxy, but only those who have suffered long could even bear to face their import.

Adversity does indeed seem to be the common lot of all people who make their mark in the world (and indeed, I believe nearly all of us in fact). It is how we bear this adversity that determines not only the success of our lives, but also what we bequeath to those that follow us. The real villains of history have so often been highly 'religious' people or scheming, successful politicians, who have been able to pervert the ways of the common people; in the twentieth century we have seen far too many examples of this to call for more detailed comment. The success of a frankly evil system like Nazism and the much more plausible but equally obnoxious excesses of some Communistic states are probably the most terrible examples of this trend. Those that follow begin to learn a vital fact that we all get the government that we deserve.

It had been said that for evil to succeed all that is required is that good people do nothing. A friend does not come into this category; when they see their friend in danger they respond immediately, and even to the detriment of their own prosperity will come and protect that person. In other words, friendship acts and is not merely a state of goodwill towards other people. Self-sacrifice, which we have considered on a number of occasions, is an essential element of friendship; it may not necessarily always be a radical offering of one's life, but a true friend would immediately show themself ready for the summons. One of the smaller Christian denominations, the Quakers, is described as the Society of Friends and they often greet each other as 'friend'. Certainly, their overall reputation has been exceptional and they have led the way in many social reforms, the most notable of which was the abolition of slavery.

When one considers family life, one vital element is often neglected. This is friendship between the various members of the group. Whether a marriage ultimately succeeds or not depends on the degree of friendship between husband and wife; gone, thank God, are the days when the man was automatically the ruler of the household and his wife and children merely servants to his wishes. On the other hand, there is a school of thought, by no means to be disregarded, that is critical of a society in which discipline is a word to be scorned, if not absolutely shunned. This view reminds us that there is a hierarchical structure to the community which is natural to most people, but provided that structure is cemented by bonds of friendship, it will emerge entire and better formed than if everyone is completely free to go their own way. Happiness is contingent on the friendship, but people do not need to sacrifice their own identity in order to achieve it. Therefore, discipline is also an essential part of happiness, but that discipline has to involve the person themself and this can be extremely difficult. Like all the other virtues, it does not develop overnight, but is the result of deep self-knowledge with many pains in its evolution.

Humanity is seldom able to strike the middle way between extremes; the authoritarian way of extreme discipline, and here I am thinking particularly of governments, is in due course replaced by a liberal establishment in which every aberration is regarded as acceptable. This in turn is followed by a reversal of attitudes to extreme discipline with its own inhibitory effect. Humanity will truly have come of age when it learns that the great gift of freedom comes into its own only when it is closely guarded by the reverence of alert people who care not only for each other but also for a higher truth, which is one way in which God may be understood. It is sad to reflect that God in this nature is not always recognized, even by people who pride themselves on their particular religious affiliation, because they all claim to be possessors of the real truth. It is only through personal growth in the midst of persistent adversity that we may transcend the boundaries of individual desire to a state of selfless concern for the world at large. Then alone do we enter the portals of happiness. When we are nothing and have nothing further to lose, we are able to contain the whole universe and even know the nature of God who is above all else perfect love.

The converse of friendship, at least in a social context, is loneliness. This is a distinctly depressing state of feeling solitary and companionless, and the isolation can indeed be hard to bear. There are two basic factors that predispose to loneliness, the character of the person themself and the society in which they live. Some people have a naturally gregarious tendency and make friends with almost everyone they see. On the surface this would appear to be very fortunate, but like everything else, it too has its darker side. The contacts whom the gregarious type of person calls friends may be very superficial indeed so that neither party remembers the other for any great length of time. The great fear inherent in the gregarious person is the barely conceivable situation of being completely alone. This is not admirable, because as one learns in the course of one's life, there are not a few situations at the other extreme when one has to rely entirely on one's own power of survival. The worst examples have been seen in our own century when people have been isolated on religious or racial grounds. One might believe that they would have the support at least of fellow sufferers, but in fact suffering of this intensity tends to drive the individual inwards so that they become less rather than more communicative, even with those of their own kind. It all depends, for there are some Holocaust victims who were loved by their whole community before their own inevitable extermination. In the milder forms of loneliness the person is either extremely introverted by nature, or else is isolated from the main community by being 'foreign'. It can be extremely difficult for such a naturally reserved individual to enter into the larger community until some innately kinder person takes them under their wing and introduces them to other people. This is one of the traumatic experiences of emigration, but in the end it is not to be avoided. If one survives, as is usually the case, one grows in strength, sympathy and understanding of other people and can become a far finer world citizen as a result. Therefore loneliness is not the opposite of friendship but rather that of friendliness. We all, I believe, are bound to experience both of these qualities in our lives.

Another quality that appears to be closely akin to friendship is popularity. This is a faculty of being liked and admired by people generally. What on the surface appears to be very closely linked to friendship is in fact distinctly different from it. The types of people who are particularly popular in our mass-communication age are media performers, politicians (of the correct persuasion, of course), charismatic religious leaders and sportsmen and women. Most of the 'fans' of these people have never met them as individuals – if they had, it is by no means improbable that they would soon have become very disenchanted – but their image remains in the mind, as these people represent special qualities that the masses particularly admire and would like to emulate. The main difference between friendship and popularity is surely that while true friendship remains and matures through experience, popularity attains its peak very rapidly but after a relatively short period of dominance it may descend dramatically into nothing, or even a negative quality, when the object of admiration is seen, like the rest of us, to have feet of clay. It is not for nothing that Jesus said 'Alas for you when all speak well of you; that is how their fathers treated the false prophets' (Luke 6:26). In other words, the great mass of people are very fickle, and if any of us have even a few real friends we should consider ourselves extremely fortunate. We all, I hope, have a stream of pleasant acquaintances whom we know quite well and meet from time to time, but without the degree of intimacy included in a true friendship. There would not be the intensity of warmth or the degree of trust found in a real friend.

Allied to this view of popularity is the way that many people treat someone who is particularly useful in their own lives at a particular time. When all is going well, there is a 'hail-fellow-well-met' attitude, but as soon as the individual appears to lose their usefulness, they are quite spontaneously dropped. They are friends as long as they can be of use to the other person. This is a more deliberate way of illustrating the same quality, how few of us could bear the depth of character revealed by a really searching relationship that called upon the exposure of the full extent of our inner resources. People who tend to name-drop usually have little conception of the meaning of genuine friendship.

The quality of friendship is intimately connected with our character. Friendly qualities include trustworthiness, consideration for others and generosity of heart. A person who is a friend should be more than merely a personal support; they should have a warmth of feeling for the greater world. Intimate friendships are, of course, of vital importance, particularly when the question of love and marriage are concerned. But friendship is always incomplete when it is limited to individuals. Supposing I, for instance, were to fall out with somebody for what I regard as a very good reason; should a true friend follow my course and support me also? I personally would hope not. Friends though we may be, we also have our own personal lives to lead, and just as it would be wrong for me to hope that you would concur with my political or artistic views, so it would be equally wrong of me to want you to tailor your coat according to my cloth. Unity should be the order of all relationships, but once uniformity becomes paramount, the individuality of the person is compromised. All this is obvious enough to a person well schooled in life and to those spiritually sensitive also; of course each person's approach to God is determined by their own character. The end is common but the means of approaching it are inevitably unique. If we attempt to change our approach according to the demands of other people, the results are always false and in the end our objective is not the highest good so much as pleasing other people by demonstrating that we are made in their mould. This is the basis of dictatorship; anyone involved in family counselling recognizes its nature only too clearly, and the dictatorial one is always completely unaware of the havoc they are causing. It is not for nothing that our way of relating to other people demonstrates most closely our own character, and what we see is seldom completely complimentary. If I were to consider friendship in the more mature context, I would see that as one grows in experience so one can genuinely include a variety of different people in its context. The very variation in character of our numerous friends indicates how well we ourselves have developed, and that we are less restricted by personal and social prejudices so that we can accept people as individuals in their own right and no longer enforce pre-conditions on our relationships. These always develop in ways that we do not expect; this is what makes life so interesting and at the same time so frustrating. But if we can weather the storm, we are coming very close to experiencing true happiness.

Friendships in the Bible

The most outstanding friendship recorded in the Old Testament begins at 1 Samuel 18:1–4, after David had killed the Philistine giant Goliath directly with a single stone from his sling.

> That same day, when Saul had finished talking with David, he kept him and would not let him return any more to his father's house, for he saw that Jonathan had given his heart to David and had grown to love him as himself. Jonathan and David made a solemn compact because each loved the other as dearly as himself. Jonathan stripped off the cloak and tunic he was wearing, and gave them to David, together with his sword, his bow, and his belt.

The subsequent adventures of Jonathan and David and the increasing animosity of Saul embrace the final chapters of the first book of Samuel, ending at Chapter 31. The picture is that of two very young men seen so frequently as comic-strip characters in our modern entertainments industry. Saul's animosity followed the triumphant acclaim of the women of Israel; 'Saul struck down thousands, but David tens of thousands'. As a result, Saul began to fear and therefore to hate David more and more and planned his destruction; there is almost certainly an aspect of paranoid psychosis in the intense antipathy of Saul. At any rate, the book ends with the defeat of the Israelite army by the Philistines in the course of which both Saul and Jonathan were killed; David escaped because he was outlawed by Saul during this period. The second book of Samuel contains the most famous dirge in the Bible: David's lament over Saul and Jonathan:

> Israel, upon your heights your beauty lies slain!
> How are the warriors fallen!

> Do not tell it in Gath or proclaim it in the streets of Ashkelon,
> in case the Philistine maidens rejoice,
> and the daughters of the uncircumcised exult.
> Hills of Gilboa, let no dew or rain fall on you,

no showers on the uplands!
For there the shields of the warriors lie tarnished,
and the shield of Saul, no longer bright with oil.
The bow of Jonathan never held back
from the breast of the foeman, from the blood of the slain;
The sword of Saul never returned
empty to the scabbard.

Beloved and lovely were Saul and Jonathan;
neither in life nor in death were they parted.
They were swifter than eagles,
stronger than lions.
Daughters of Israel, weep for Saul,
who clothed you in scarlet and rich embroideries,
who spangled your attire with jewels of gold.

How are the warriors fallen on the field of battle!
Jonathan lies slain on your heights.
I grieve for you, Jonathan, my brother;
you were most dear to me;
your love for me was wonderful,
surpassing the love of women.

How are the warriors fallen,
and their armour abandoned on the battlefield!

(2 Samuel 1:19–27)

The beauty of this poem is enhanced by David's spontaneous warmth of affection towards Saul, who not so long before had planned his murder while he was still a fugitive. In fact, if one sees the tragedy in a wider light, the magnanimity of David is outstanding, and it is no wonder that he remains the prototype of a great Jewish leader.

When one comes to the New Testament, there is no comparable instance of great friendship on this level. The eleven apostles who supported Jesus (this, of course, excludes Judas Iscariot who betrayed him) were faceless individuals at the time of the Incarnation. Only at the time of the Acts of the Apostles do they grow into real people and their friendship is assumed rather than described. It seems as if they largely went on their own particular ways to proclaim the new gospel, and indeed the essential proclaimer of the faith, Saul of Tarsus, was not one of their number and only gradually grew into fellowship with them, since he started his career as a persecutor of the new religion.

It is very doubtful whether religious affinity has a great deal to do with personal friendship of the type that I have described in this chapter. Much more often religion is the breeding ground of discord and hatred, not only amongst those with contrary religious views but even more tragically among those who identify themselves with a particular religion. The usual cause of discord and hatred is doctrinal inflexibility, each group knowing that they are the possessors of the only truth. It is little surprise, therefore, that religion divides at least as often as it unites – except perhaps in a time of emergency.

6 Love and its variations

Love is usually described as an intense emotional attraction with a corresponding physical involvement between two people, in the great majority of instances a man and a woman. The term's use is often extended beyond personal relationships to include a strong partiality to an inanimate object like a food or a pastime, such as a sport or hobby. All this illustrates the perennial human tendency to degrade a sacred quality by frequent ill-considered usage. The sublime is closer to the ridiculous than many people would care to consider. Human love has a physical aspect that sets it apart from a very noble friendship. But then what are we to make of the farewell discourses ascribed to Jesus in chapters 13 to 16 of the Fourth Gospel? 'I give you a new commandment: Love one another; as I have loved you, so you are to love one another. If there is love among you, then everyone will know that you are my disciples' (John 13:34–35). This is a typical example of what Christian love should entail. Its depth should aspire to the profundity of John 15:13, 'There is no greater love than this, that someone should lay down his life for his friends.' This is the supreme apotheosis of friendship, reaching the utmost height of self-dedication, but the less intense love seen in usual human relationships has a strongly physical aspect, especially when the couple are young. In older people the balance may slant more towards emotional warmth as the physical activity wanes.

The most famous writing on love is Chapter 13 of St Paul's first letter to the Corinthians. One could quite easily devote the whole of this chapter to an analysis of the various points he makes, but to me three aspects are particularly outstanding. In the first three sentences he sees that love is greater than any language, whether of men or of angels, that it surpasses the gift of prophecy, the knowledge of truth and even sufficient faith to move mountains. Finally, even giving all one possesses to the poor to the extent of giving one's very body to be burned, is useless if there is no love behind it. This is a particularly extreme statement because even so-called charity on a large scale is useless if it is not given with a loving heart. We speak sometimes of a person being as cold as charity for a very good reason; they give with the condescension which comes from a person who is both grudging and feels superior to poorer people.

The next important point is that love will never come to an end; prophecies may cease, tongues of ecstasy fall silent and knowledge itself fall silent, but love will remain until the end of time. The final point follows on this observation, knowledge grows. 'When I was a child I spoke like a child, thought like a child, reasoned like a child; but when I grew up I finished with childish things. At present we see only puzzling reflections in a mirror, but one day we shall see face to face. My knowledge now is partial; then it will be whole, like God's knowledge of me' (1 Corinthians 13:11–12). From this we can deduce that when we really love a person we know that person and, as I mentioned in Chapter 3, this requires self-knowledge also. Here we see the great difference between desire and love. The two are frequently and mistakenly equated, but in fact they are very different indeed. Love gives of itself to the other, whereas desire wants for itself. In terms of sexual activity love culminates in joyful self-giving, whereas desire moves insidiously into lust and even rape.

Our age is one in which such values are not merely disregarded but are frequently derided. It would be far better if people could learn the wise practice of self-control; the current counsel is, however, that we should not repress our feelings; this is wise as long as we are educated in social behaviour. One certainly should not repress any feelings in oneself in so far as one dare not face their private acknowledgement, but the advisability of their public expression is very much governed by the common good. We may have whatever views we like about the desirability of different types of sexual activity, but it is always essential that children and those who are defenceless through mental illness should be protected against predators or being taken advantage of by the Don Juan type of individual. In the end the child has to make up their own mind and live according to their own proclivities; a person's sexual preference is very much their own business and should be private and sacred to them.

There is certainly a proper way of sexual behaviour: chastity or else a faithful marriage should be the choice open to the responsible type of individual, but in such a fluid society as that of the present time it is far wiser to remain silent and listen to other points of view than to sit on a self-appointed throne and dole out morality to those whom one considers weaker brethren. Judgement is pleasant when we can assume the role of prosecuting counsel but less so when we are the defendant. At present there is a powerful school of thought that sexual experience should be mandatory before the couple are married, and there is obviously much sense in this view. I have known a number of instances when the husband has been impotent from the nuptial night and remained so subsequently. In these cases the wife has tolerated the situation bitterly, and many such wives would have arranged a separation forthwith. Indeed, I doubt whether a contemporary couple would allow the situation to drag on at all; the instances I quoted were married many years ago, and the wife was fond of her impotent husband as well as flinching from divorce proceedings.

Yet there is more to marriage that mere sexual satisfaction, which after all can be obtained quite as easily (and far less expensively) in a casual or temporary way. The extra dimension of a real marriage is love. This is the basis of stability as well as the permanency of marriage. In *The Tablet* (a Roman Catholic weekly) an important article entitled 'Sex is for life' appeared in the 2 May 1998 issue on page 542. The writer is Jack Dominian, an eminent psychiatrist and author of numerous books on marriage and sexuality. The gist of his article is that sexual intercourse arises out of a combination of a capacity to give and receive affection, coupled with physical sexual attraction. Unless there is a deep underlying love, there will be little likelihood of a marriage lasting very long. The love of which I write is founded basically on our relationship with our parents; this is our first experience of love, and the success of the sexual function depends on this love. A purely physical attraction often tends to diminish in the course of time, especially in women, but in a real marriage the underlying love remains unbowed; it flows out to the children, who perpetuate it in their own lives. The great majority of sexual inadequacies in both men and women are of psychological origin.

Conjugal love

I confess that as a natural celibate having no experience of this subject I am largely unqualified to write about it. Nevertheless my experience in counselling a considerable number of people, and more important my own life's experience, give me material that I feel is worth sharing. To me the great difference between a deep friendship and a marriage relationship lies in its permanency associated with living under one roof. Friends necessarily live according to the circumstances of life even when their close connection does not falter, but partners are bound spiritually, and in the case of husband and wife legally also, to one another. This is the real test of love. Will it survive the inevitable changes and chances of mortal existence for better or for worse, for richer or for poorer, when there is disease or only in health, and indeed when the whole world seems to be falling apart in the lives of the two committed individuals? A friendship is not subject to this degree of intense testing. Sometimes it may grow quite dim because one of the friends may have work to do which keeps them apart from the other for quite a long time, but when they communicate again, perhaps before Christmas or some other festive occasion like a birthday celebration, the warmth is immediately restored and the people greet one another with the same degree of cordiality as they did at the beginning of their friendship.

Husband and wife do not have this convenient degree of latitude; they are bound together by ties of responsibility. If one is ill, it is not merely the duty but the deep concern of the other to afford assistance, so that health and security may be restored. Married life is not one in which the participants subsequently 'live happily ever after'. There is bound to be turmoil; this is not an indication of the superficiality of the relationship so much as the opportunity afforded to each partner to grow in self-knowledge and caring.

In a marriage relationship some discord is inevitable, because both partners have to 'work out their own salvation with fear and trembling' (Philippians 2:12). Even if a relationship has of necessity to slacken, it is important that there is still an underlying feeling of fondness and concern. This is the basic responsibility of marriage, that the partners stick together despite even major disagreements. The value of this is obvious in that it teaches us to realize that there are other points of view besides our own, and that often the wisest way is silence and listening rather than laying down our own law according to a moral precept which is very much in keeping with our own situation. Morality is always pleasant when you are on the right side, but less so when others cite conflicting views. The great lesson learnt from marriage is tolerance, and it is for this reason that I dislike divorce, unless the situation is so unacceptable that separation becomes inevitable.

The essential corollary of marital responsibility is self-control. In practice, however, each of the couple is liable to have 'affairs', but experience has taught me, the outsider, that it is far better if the two can face their frailty and decide to live together rather than to separate indefinitely. In this statement there is a clear difference between terminating a friendship and ending a marriage. The legal and spiritual requirements of marriage are not easily revoked, and very often children are also involved. Their education and happiness should be a burning issue that drives husband and wife closer together, even if there may be many points of disagreement between them in their relationship. One does not need to have a physical relationship in order to fulfil a marriage, but such a relationship is extremely desirable apart from the satisfaction it affords both partners; its ultimate consummation is the birth of a new soul into the world.

An abortion is in my opinion highly undesirable unless there are the strongest medical grounds for the termination of the pregnancy. My own mother, a remarkably beautiful woman, had an abortion in the early 1920s for purely social reasons. She soon suffered, as do the great majority of women who have had abortions, on an emotional and spiritual level. A very severe depression followed this frivolous abortion, and when I was born (a boy like the aborted foetus), my mother was much more neurotic than she had been before this destructive act had been performed. I suffered severely through her neurotic temperament; although I have no doubt that she loved me intensely, she could not control her fiery, unpredictable temper and screamed on the most trivial occasions. She also had terrible rows with her relatives, which often ended in a complete break in relationships that on occasion lasted many years. This resulted in my becoming distanced from my cousins at the same time. As an only child my loneliness was very considerable. Our African servants (I spent the first 24 years of my life in South Africa) suffered particularly from her ill humour.

As a counsellor, I am not infrequently confronted with a situation of a man or woman, perhaps already married for a number of years, who has met the woman or man who really understands them. They still love their spouse in their own particular way, but it is the new star who lightens up their life and gives him or her a real reason for living. What is to be done? My own experience, completely free of prejudice, has taught me that in the majority of cases the marriage should be sustained, but there are instances where the couple drift so inexorably apart that a separation is inevitable.

Married life is not simply a journey for two people on a pleasant steamboat; it is one in which both of them are required to develop their own personalities with their accompanying talents. True love does not require uniformity; indeed, such a situation can lead to stagnation and intolerance of others who have other points of view. Love, in other words, has its inevitable ups and downs. This is a somewhat circuitous way of saying that we are most real when we forget ourselves and give of what we are to others. Then at last do we become real people. 'Whoever gains his life will lose it; but whoever loses his life for my sake will gain it' (Matthew 10:39).

This rather obscure statement, which is the key to so much of Jesus' teaching, depends on the higher understanding of life. The life of the unreflective person, which is centred on themselves and their own desires, has inevitably to come to its end with the processes of ageing, disease and finally death itself. On the other hand, the spiritually illuminated individual who has seen the futile pettiness of life as it is generally lived and knows something of the nature of the soul where Christ is recognized, begins to experience a new dimension of living in which the ego, or personality, becomes the servant rather than assuming its usual role as master. The serving self is identical to the soul and indeed can never be destroyed. The fortunate ones among us have at least glimpsed this truth and at once their lives become implicit with meaning, as I learnt in my recent near-death experience. It is on this level that loving relationships have a permanency that will outlast the trends of the times.

Life is our most precious gift, and on it the destiny of the human race depends. No life is without its usefulness, the tragedy being that some people use their lives well while others squander them on trivialities and vices. It is at this level that religion will always play a vital role, not only in the progress of our species but also in its survival. We consider this in greater detail in Chapter 7.

A biblical marriage

The meeting of Isaac and Rebecca (Rebekah) is a beautifully impressionistic account of two people destined to carry out God's will in providing descendants for the people of Israel (Genesis 24). Abraham's wife, Sarah, had died some little time before, and under no condition did he want Isaac to marry into the local community. He therefore ordered his servant to return to his family who lived in Upper Mesopotamia in order to find a suitable wife for his son. When the servant reached his destination he saw some women from the town going to a spring to collect water. An inner urge made him pray directly to God that his mission would be successful and that the right woman would manifest herself.

> He said, 'I would say to the girl, please lower your jar so that I may drink, and if she answers, "Drink and I shall water your camels also", let that be the girl whom you intend for your servant Isaac. In this way, I shall know that you have kept faith with my master.'
>
> Before he had finished praying he saw Rebecca coming out with her water-jar on her shoulder. She was the daughter of Bethuel, son of Milcah, the wife of Abraham's brother Nahor. The girl was very beautiful and a virgin. She went down to the spring, filled her jar and came up again. Abraham's servant hurried to meet her and said, 'Will you give me a little water from your jar?' 'Please drink, sir,' she answered, and at once lowered her jar on to her hand to let him drink. When she had finished giving him a drink, she said, 'I shall draw water for your camels also until they have had enough.' She quickly emptied her jar into the water trough, and then hurrying again to the well she drew water and watered all the camels.
>
> The man was watching quietly to see whether the Lord had made his journey successful, and when the camels had finished drinking, he took a gold nose ring, and two bracelets for her wrists. 'Tell me, please, whose daughter you are', he said. 'Is there room in your father's house for us to spend the night?'

She recounted her immediate ancestry, and also said that there was plenty of straw and fodder and also room for him to spend the night. So the man bowed down and prostrated himself before God.

> The girl ran to her mother's house and told them what had happened. Rebecca had a brother named Laban who, after seeing the nose ring and the bracelets on his sister's wrists and hearing her account of what had been said to her, hurried out to the spring. When he arrived he found the man still standing by the camels.

He promptly invited him in with the camels, but he would not eat until he had delivered his message. He recounted Abraham's great wealth with many animals, and also his assignation to find a wife for his son from his own family's descendants and not from the women of the Canaanites in whose land he was at present living. Abraham had promised that the Lord would send an angel to make his journey successful, but if the woman refused to leave her family the servant would be released from the charge that had been laid upon him by Abraham. Also if he came to the family and they refused to give her to him, the servant would likewise be released from the charge.

The servant recounted his meeting with Rebecca and asked quite frankly whether the family meant to deal loyally and faithfully with Isaac. If not, they should say so and he would turn elsewhere.

> Laban and Bethuel replied, 'Since this is from the Lord, we can say nothing for or against it. Here is Rebecca, take her and go, she shall be the wife of your master's son, as the Lord has decreed.' When Abraham's servant heard what they said, he prostrated himself on the ground before the Lord. Then he brought out silver and gold ornaments and articles of clothing, and gave them to Rebecca, and he gave costly gifts to her brother and her mother. Only then did he and his men eat and drink and spend the night there. When they rose in the morning Abraham's servant said, 'Give me leave to return to my master.' Rebecca's brother and her mother replied that the girl should stay with them for a few days and then go, but he said, 'Do not detain me, for it is the Lord who has granted me success. Give

me leave to go back to my master.' The family decided that Rebecca herself should be asked and she answered, 'Yes, I will go.' So they let their sister Rebecca and her maid go with Abraham's servant and his men. They blessed Rebecca and said to her: 'You are our sister, may you be the mother of many children; may your sons possess the cities of your enemies.' Rebecca and her companions mounted their camels to follow the man, and so the servant took Rebecca and set out.

Isaac meanwhile had moved on as far as Beer-Lahai-Roi and was living in the Negeb. One evening when he had gone out into the open country hoping to meet them, he looked and saw camels approaching. When Rebecca saw Isaac, she dismounted from her camel, saying to the servant, 'Who is that man walking across the open country towards us?' When the servant answered, 'It is my master', she took her veil and covered herself. The servant related to Isaac all that had happened. Isaac conducted her into the tent and took her as his wife. So she became his wife and he loved her, and was consoled for the death of his mother Sarah.

In the great triad of Israelite patriarchs Isaac stands between Abraham and Jacob. He is the least colourful of the three in his actions, but he provided an essential link in the chain that led to the history of the chosen people and from them to Jesus himself.

Homosexual love

Society has always had its marginalized people. These have at various times included women, Jews, gypsies, 'foreigners' but above all those with homosexual tendencies, nowadays called 'gay'. One remembers with sadness the terrible persecution that Oscar Wilde had to bear at the end of the nineteenth century. Now, a hundred years later, a kinder and much more informed attitude has developed in relation to male homosexuality – female homosexuality (lesbianism), though frowned on, has never been a criminal offence as was the male variety until about thirty years ago. Union with one's own sex is obviously not the most common form of love, but I doubt whether it is anybody else's business to pry into the sexual lives of their fellows. That there is a decidedly acceptable aspect of male homosexuality has become obvious to previous detractors by the marvellous devotion shown to many AIDS victims by their life partners. A devotion of this depth deserves to be called 'love', and in as much as all love is of God, homosexual love has its divine nature also. The public at large has learnt to accept homosexuality as a variation rather than merely an aberration, and this in my opinion is as it ought to be. One's own private prejudices are as sacred as one's sexuality, and I personally would not want to convert anybody to my particular views. As I have written on more than one occasion elsewhere, we become most authentic as people when we forget ourselves entirely and do the work at hand as well as we can. My own view is that the great majority of gay people are born that way from the time of conception; it is part of their destiny, another matter which is discussed in Chapter 10.

Celibacy

A celibate is a person who has always been single or who has deliberately embraced singleness. This may be through some physical inadequacy or be as natural as marriage or homosexual union. I certainly was born celibate and I knew this at a very early age. Can a celibate love? Celibacy certainly may be the precursor of monumental selfishness but it is also the way to supreme self-giving. The two greatest religious geniuses who have inspired humanity, Gautama and Jesus, did their spiritual work in a celibate state, Jesus, as far as we know, from the time of his birth, and Gautama when he knew that he had to find enlightenment.

Natural celibacy is undoubtedly a grace, even if the loneliness that is a part of its burden may be hard to bear in a world of garish exhibitionism. It certainly makes for a solitary type of existence, especially in one who does not make friends easily. Indeed, only in my later years have I acquired a circle of loving people whom I really can consider my friends. But I have gained something far greater: the capacity to bear loneliness and to appreciate my own company without in any way feeling different from others.

Life is basically an experience of loneliness. Even those who are happily married have to face the ultimate challenge of ageing, the death of their partner, and the growth of their children into mature adults who have their own lives to lead and their own families to care for. The right way is that older members should be placed under the protective family wing, and in any loving family this protective function would be assumed. It is unfortunate when people who are old have to be lodged in a residential home, but circumstances may make this inevitable.

It is little wonder that I do not regard my basic loneliness, which has been so well borne, with bitterness but rather with increasing gratitude. The natural habitat for people of my temperament is a monastic order, and I have the highest regard for these institutions, irrespective of their religious affiliation. But there are some, like myself, who do not fit well into any community because of our individualistic tendency. Being a member of no community, I am a world citizen and have, at least so far, survived very well in this climate. No one knows what the future holds for any of us, but the near-death experience which I have described has shown me it is how we live our lives in the present that matters in the relatively short time that we have left on this earth. It is for this reason that I abstain from judging the way of life of other people, provided it does not interfere with the public good.

Celibacy has positive advantages apart from what I have already described. While its danger is self-centredness, its advantage lies in a life that can be devoted fully to the concern of one's fellow creatures. If one leads the sort of life that I have described in Chapter 2 with regard to my work of healing and counselling, one enters unobtrusively into the lives of many other people in a way that is not interfering or dominating. I know very few people like this who have attained what I would call true celibate status. In my experience, the most dangerous individual is one who is 'good' and really does mean well; compared with such a person, the out-and-out rogue is small beer. The rogue is obvious and causes only limited damage, whereas the good person cannot avoid interfering with the lives of many others, naturally, for their own good! Of course, this is a pure illusion, but the amount of anger and disturbance they can occasion is immense. A celibate would be very unlikely to work in this ignorant, self-assured fashion for they would know through their own sensitivity how to respect the privacy of other people. This, I believe, is the heart of celibacy, being so self-possessed that one can give freely of oneself to others without looking for rewards. If one has a family, one's allegiance must naturally be devoted to one's own; after all, this is the whole point of family life. If, on the other hand, one owns nothing other than one's immediate possessions, which are unlikely to be excessive, one can really spend one's time profitably in helping a large number of people. I doubt whether my life would have been any more profitable or happier had I been married.

Ending on a psychological note, it was obvious from the very beginning that I would never marry because of my dysfunctional family – I have already discussed my mother's temperament. My father was kind but worldly and unimaginative, and I had no siblings. I could hardly avoid having a lack of confidence with its concurrent low self-esteem, but as I describe further in Chapter 10, I believe this was my destiny from the very time of my conception. I am well aware of the psychoanalytic theories of Freud and his numerous successors. My final conclusion is that one is wise to study them; and take much of what they contain with a grain of salt. Such theories as *sublimation* (the Freudian concept of transforming our weaknesses into alternative means of strength or else products of art or culture) and the Adlerian idea of simple *compensation* (weaknesses acting as a stimulus for later unusual individual development) are inadequate to account for the unique aspects of individual character. Jung's theories are more acceptable because they give due regard to suprarational factors in personality development.

Love on a larger scale

> I vow to thee, my country – all earthly things above
> Entire and whole and perfect, the service of my love.
> (Sir Cecil Arthur Spring-Rice (1858–1918), 'The Last Poem')

These well-known lines remind us that love is more than merely personal but involves large numbers of people, particularly those who live in our own particular country. This love of one's native land is called patriotism and is exalted not only in magnificent poetry but by the way many young lives have been spent and lost in its defence. The two World Wars of the twentieth century have illustrated this in no uncertain way. But as great empires have fallen and their constituent parts have emerged as separate countries, so patriotism should become more universal. When a country emerges into independence the feeling of its inhabitants is one of nationalism. If one studies the history of the unification of Italy and Germany in the nineteenth century, one notices that as separate states united to form a great country so there was a liberalization of policy and a mighty force emerged. In the case of Germany it was the Prussian state that ultimately took control. Patriotism is certainly a fine quality provided it is contained in an admiration and concern for other countries also. Unfortunately as the World Wars already alluded to have shown, patriotism can move beyond concern for one's own country to a lust to dominate others as well. Thus nationalism is an essential precursor of patriotism but while it remains dominant, patriotism is never perfect.

I think particularly of my native country South Africa. Cape Town was colonized originally in the seventeenth century by the Dutch, but at the end of the eighteenth and throughout the nineteenth centuries the British took possession of the Cape Province and Natal. The Afrikaners, the descendants of the original Dutch people as they were then called, pioneered inwards – they were the 'voortrekkers' into what was to become the two other provinces of South Africa, the Orange Free State and the Transvaal. Towards the end of the nineteenth century gold was discovered in the southern Transvaal; the Witwatersrand including Johannesburg was founded in 1886, and it was inevitable that the British would cast their eyes on this possession also. This occurred at the very height of the British Empire. Now at last South Africa was part of that empire and bitter hatred developed between the Afrikaner boer (farmer) and the British invader. Meanwhile both sides treated the black inhabitants, who were there long before the white invasion, quite literally like dirt. They were of course of great value, particularly in the goldmines. The present history is illuminating. Shortly after the end of the Second World War the Afrikaner Nationalist Party gained ascendancy and maintained it. In the 1950s they introduced the system of 'apartheid' which meant a complete separation of black and white communities, with severe penal measures against anyone who contravened this draconian law.

I spent the first 24 years of my life in South Africa where I studied medicine, coming to England only in 1951. I came here to acquire higher medical degrees, having received my basic medical training in South Africa. It was while I was doing National Service that apartheid was instituted. Looking on then, as a British citizen and therefore essentially an observer, I could see only too clearly what was in store for this beautiful yet horribly misguided country. The gross injustice of apartheid inflamed world opinion as well as that of more sensitive, decent white South Africans, and in due course the long-exiled (27 years imprisoned) Nelson Mandela was brought back from Robben Island (near Cape Town), and made president of a country that truly represented the needs of the great majority of the population, who obviously were black and coloured people. But what I expected was a subsequent bloodbath; that this has not so far come about is a great tribute to the Christian qualities of the new leaders of South Africa. One thinks here especially (in addition to Mandela) of Archbishop Desmond Tutu, the Anglican Primate of the country and Bishop Trevor Huddleston, an Anglican religious from Mirfield in Yorkshire, who earlier on fought passionately for black African rights and died in 1998. There is unfortunately a prevalence of violent crime at the moment, but this could hardly be avoided as part of the teething problems of a young emerging country.

It is obvious that love has allowed this amazing sequence of events, in my opinion a miracle, to take place, and we all pray that peace may continue in this way and a society may emerge in which black and white may come together in friendship and co-operation. Certainly, the absence of an outbreak of revenge on the part of the black and coloured population is quite remarkable.

A last consideration

The last matter concerning love is involved in the human will, which is the capacity to bring to fulfilment the desire of the heart. This is more than something that is forced on us, but rather the activity of the true Self or soul. It is active in all of us, though it makes itself known in only a few. The saying 'God helps those who help themselves' has a degree of truth; it is the soul that makes the activity of God open to us, and it is that soul also which has made the great religions of the world survive, despite the horrifying cruelty committed in their name by some of their votaries. I suspect, however, that the devil himself has had his part to play in our growth to maturity, for he too is a member of the court of heaven, as we read in Job 1:6 where he is described as the Adversary, Satan. This is, of course, merely an allegory, but it tells us that evil itself, in a way that we dare hardly consider at the moment, has its part to play in humanity's growth to its fullness. This is something of the history of Christ himself, the mystery of mysteries. There would have been no resurrection without the prior crucifixion. Not only was the Lord killed but the disciples were shriven of all their illusions. Only a little while before, James and John, Zebedee's sons, had desired special seats at the heavenly table (Matthew 20:20–23).

I feel the last word on love should go to Shakespeare; he says such delightful things about it in Sonnet 141:

In faith, I do not love thee with mine eyes,
for they in thee a thousand errors note;
But 'tis my heart that loves what they despise,
Who, in despite of view, is pleased to dote.
Nor are mine ears with thy tongue's tune delighted;
Nor tender feeling to base touches prone,
Nor taste, nor smell, desire to be invited
To any sensual feast with thee alone:
But my five wits nor my five senses can
Dissuade one foolish heart from serving thee,
Who leaves unswayed the likeness of a man,
Thy proud heart's slave and vassal wretch to be:
 Only my plague thus far I count my gain,
 That she that makes me sin awards me pain.

7 Spirituality and religion

From what has already been said, it becomes increasingly apparent that the things of this world do not ultimately satisfy the soul even when they are in excess, but what is the soul? It is an inner awareness that we all have but not all of us actually acknowledge. It knows what is right for us and what is most decidedly inadequate. This is not exactly the same as a sense of morality, which may be defined as the capacity to distinguish between right and wrong. Morality is an excellent quality, but it is ultimately dictated by the *mores* of any age. It is interesting, for instance, to see that in most Western European countries, and certainly Britain, capital punishment has been abolished (though it is still very much a factor in the USA).

Even in our own generation our attitude to sexual irregularities has been much liberalized. I am decidedly for liberalization, and believe that people are born in the great majority of instances with their own particular sexual traits. Who am I as a natural celibate, for instance, to turn my nose up at gay people while accepting the 'normal' heterosexual who quite often has a hard-hearted attitude to others? I am saying in fact that what matters is the overall character of the individual rather than their sexual orientation.

The more secure one is in oneself, the easier it is to accept other people for what they are and to desist from criticizing them. Jesus in one of his most telling parables compares two people, a self-righteous Pharisee and a tax-collector.

Both of them went to the Temple to pray. The Pharisee stood up and made this prayer, 'I thank you, God, that I am not like the rest of mankind – greedy, dishonest, adulterous – or, for that matter, like this tax-collector, I fast twice a week; I pay tithes on all that I get.' But the other kept his distance and would not even raise his eyes to heaven, but beat on his breast, saying, 'God, have mercy on me, sinner that I am.' It was this man, I tell you, and not the other who went home acquitted of his sins. For everyone who exalts himself will be humbled; and whoever humbles himself will be exalted. (Luke 18:10–14)

This episode is followed by an account of babies being brought to Jesus for him to touch them.

The disciples rebuked those who brought the children, but Jesus called the children and said, 'Let the children come to me; do not try to stop them; for the kingdom of God belongs to such as these. Truly I tell you: whoever does not accept the kingdom of God like a child will never enter it.' (Luke 18:15–17)

In these examples we can see the great difference between religion and spirituality. The essential quality of spirituality is a person's innate yearning for the Divine which is called God. This search is bound to end in failure until we come to the start of understanding that the Divine presence is closer to us that our own being, and therefore that we should look inwards through our outer experience day by day. Many people have little time for these higher thoughts because they are so immersed in the quest for money, power, health and what they call love. It is only when these idols fall about them as they did in the case of sad, completely righteous Job, that they may come to a deeper understanding of Divine reality.

Indeed, as Meister Eckhart and some of the greatest Hindu mystics have said, 'Why do you speak about God? Whatever you say is wrong.' And yet, until we are aware of the unattainable we cannot be fully aware of anything else, such is the mystery of reality. I know only one thing about myself; my mortal form and its inevitable dissolution. Interestingly enough, and very much confirmed by my recent extended near-death experience, I find both these concepts completely satisfying (and I have no death wish). When I am absolutely nothing, I begin to be myself, a self which contains everything. My celibacy, for instance, has enabled me to form links with a large number of people, perhaps for all I know, everybody, in a way that might have been less possible had I been bound exclusively to one particular individual and family only. This does not, for one moment, mean that this way of life is superior to that of a married person, but it does affirm the value of some people having a closer contact with the greater world than merely a limited family connection. Neither way is complete on its own, and as we progress in life, so our interests and understanding should broaden to include an increasing number of people. Only thus can we begin to make a contact with life as such, something that far exceeds the human personality. The personality, or ego, is how I appear to myself and to those who know me. When I am most relaxed, I am not putting on a mask, or persona, so as to impress other people. But when I have moved beyond personality so that I am indeed nothing, a deeper centre shows itself, which is in contact with all life and makes me distinctly aware of the God who cannot be defined.

> Truth is within ourselves; it takes no rise
> From outward things, whate'er you may believe.
> There is an inmost centre in us all
> Where truth abides in fulness; and around
> Wall upon wall, the gross flesh hems it in,
> This perfect, clear perception – which is truth.
> A baffling and perverting carnal mesh
> Blinds it, and makes all error, and, to *know*
> Rather consists in opening out a way
> Whence the imprisoned splendour may escape,
> Than in effecting entry for a light
> Supposed to be without.
>   (Robert Browning (1812–89), *Paracelsus*, scene 1)

This is a beautiful way of understanding the Divine nature in all that lives and comes to its highest fruition in the human soul. People like Gautama the Buddha and Jesus Christ have shown it more decisively than any others that I know, but it is a quality common to all mystics (one who seeks by contemplation and self-surrender to attain union with the Deity). Mysticism is not something that one works towards so much as a divine grace which is given, especially to those who live the good life. By this I mean a life of humility and self-giving love to all creatures. It is, incidentally, far easier to love a pet animal than a member of one's own kind, because animals, beautiful creatures as they so often may be, are dumb, whereas fellow humans may show qualities distinctly different from what we would prefer to see. Here again is an example of the human tendency to move categorically to extremes instead of sticking to the Middle Way stressed by the Buddha. This is what spirituality involves, and many that are first shall be last and the last shall be first, as Jesus taught (Matthew 19:30).

The way of spirituality involves self-control, self-knowledge and self-abasement. This is the essence of humility, and the greater the degree of soul aspiration, the more demanding is the degree of humility. When one is nothing, the divine light can truly penetrate one's personality, rendering it so translucent that it can mirror the soul, or True Self, with greater and greater perfection. The spiritual life is not an easy one, for it separates one from the usual diversions of the world. If one expects happiness from it in the usual superficial sense of the word, one is bound to be bitterly disappointed, but no one on the path to God so much as thinks along those lines. The pearl of great price becomes a radiant diamond and one's spiritual gaze is focused constantly on its presence. When one really does know this in one's heart, there is not merely happiness but, rather, complete joy.

But how does this spirituality come to one? In my case, and it is always wisest to be quite frank even if one is totally vulnerable to the charge of self-opinionation, I knew it as early as I knew myself. Detachment has always been a cardinal feature of my character because the things of this world were never cardinal in my life. I came from an indifferent middle-class background, and my father was a competent eye specialist. I was born on 30 April 1927. Both my father and my mother, who were first cousins, were of Jewish descent, and although I was frequently buffeted by the anti-Semitism of my contemporaries, I was sustained by a much deeper love which enabled me to bear race hatred, and even in an oblique way to sympathize with it. This, of course, does not mean that I approve of, or have ever approved of, racism, but merely that I have been able to understand why people dislike Jews or members of any other religious denomination foreign to themselves. I find this expression of innate prejudice, which is all too frequently confirmed by the attitudes and behaviour of individuals from whatever religious background, extremely sad.

In fact, in my case, though I had an elementary Jewish education which culminated in the confirmation ceremony called the barmitzvah at the age of thirteen, I had little fundamental deeper Jewish consciousness. This was interestingly enough fostered by the terrible events that were occurring in Nazi Germany during my childhood and adolescence. A strong group sympathy pervaded my spirituality, but I always knew inwardly that the truth could never be embraced in any one religious tradition. It was clear to me that the culmination, if not the meaning of Judaism, was included, and concluded also, in the Incarnation of Jesus of Nazareth. If you were to ask me how I knew all this, my answer would have been peculiarly unconvincing. I was a recipient of no great revelation like that of St Paul on the road to Damascus; I simply knew with an inner depth what was true. Nor did the behaviour of my Christian contemporaries especially impress me either. I have always had great respect for the Jewish way of life and Jews in general; their staying power has been incredible when one considers the terrible persecutions that they have had to endure from time immemorial, and yet I was not really one of them any more than any other specific group of people. It is interesting that I was baptized and confirmed only in 1971, long after I had started my spiritual work of counselling, healing and retreat conducting. I have to admit that I even received the Eucharist

on more than one occasion long before my formal reception
into the Christian faith as an Anglican in 1971. This would
be one of the few sins that I could reasonably confess if I
really considered it to be a sin at all, but as I have a very
open view of the love and sacrifice of Jesus, I believe that it
is one's inner attitude rather than one's outer membership of
a body that determines the power of the sacrament on the
individual.

When I was a small boy I used to converse regularly with
God whom I could not possibly describe. One book that I
have long loved has been *Mr God, This Is Anna* by an
anonymous writer who calls himself Fynn. She, like me, was
a natural mystic and could not really in her heart subscribe
absolutely to the form of any one religion. When I look back
on all this now, I can see that mystics are really universalistic
in their belief, no matter to what denomination they may
subscribe. If people were really honest, they would follow
the precepts of their particular religion, whether in the Bible,
the Koran or the wonderful writings of India or China. The
simplest of these are the Ten Commandments contained in
Exodus 20:1–17. They are so elementary that one does not
need a high degree of intelligence to understand them. How
many people in fact does one know who have not committed
murder, adultery, theft, giving false evidence or coveted the
goods or well-being of others, the last five of the Ten
Commandments? The neighbour is, in the final analysis, the
person one encounters most in the course of one's life (Luke
10:29–37). I myself have never done any of these things, not
because I am particularly good but simply because I am a
natural celibate and a mystic. St Augustine of Hippo was
certainly a great mystic, but he had an uphill fight with his
sexual desire. This is mirrored in his prayer in his *Con-
fessions*, 'Give me chastity and continence, but do not give it
yet!' Many people find this uproariously amusing, but I see
rather the great intelligence of the saint's plea. He knew
quite clearly that he had not yet attained that degree of
sanctity in which sexual desire could be raised to the level of
universal love, which is really what sex is about. In due

course his prayer was answered, and now he is one of the great Fathers of the Christian Church. This teaches one that although the spiritual gift is inborn, it grows only through the experience of powerful adverse conditions.

It is not wrong to envy or even hate someone, so long as one is aware of its impropriety and in silence gives it to God. This is in fact the very nature of prayer itself. We do not have to ask God for anything, because he knows our need even before we ourselves are aware of it. But nothing can be done until we set our mind to the quest; then alone can the vital change in our inner being slowly develop. If, on the other hand, we were to use frank, strong will-power, the results might be disastrous, especially if they appeared to be successful. The reason for this paradox is that then we would start to become like the Pharisee in the parable I have recently cited, and end up as persecutors of all the things that we personally dislike. It is for this reason that I am relieved by the slackening off of intolerant sexual morality, not because I approve of immorality but because I know that until the inner change of heart manifests itself, the hypersexed individual is less dangerous to others than they might be if they put an iron grip on their passions. Did not Jesus himself say that he of himself could do nothing, but it was the Father who was his guide, himself doing only whatever the Father did (John 5:19)?

The greatest value of religion is that it raises the degree of aspiration of anyone who takes a positive view from the things of this world to a vision of what they might be if people were to behave like true children of God. To be a child of God means in essence to resemble the Divine image as much as is possible. In fact I, like William Blake, can see the Divine image in everyone. This embraces ultimately faith, hope and love. It behoves God to have faith in what he has created and to love that even when it has failed monstrously. Hope springs eternal in the human breast (Alexander Pope, An Essay on Criticism 1, line 88), so that even when the creation appears to have failed abysmally, there is yet another chance for renewal to occur. If one takes one's religion seriously, one knows the power of forgiveness, primarily on oneself; and from that on the other individual also. Forgiveness is not simply a comfortable way of escape after bad behaviour; on the contrary, it follows a just punishment for work badly done, the sin itself producing the punishment in that it excludes the person in particular from the company of those whom they might esteem. This is a sort of personal excommunication, and its impact on the psyche can be unbearable until one has confessed one's fault, primarily to oneself and then to anyone whom one might have injured. This confession always brings healing with it, because it does not depend primarily on the attitude of the injured party but on the presence of God, who has revealed himself to one in one's own naked helplessness. Therefore, what I would call good religion is above all one that reveals the loving nature of the Creator, once we have opened ourselves to that love. 'By love may he be gotten and holden; but by thought never' (*The Cloud of Unknowing*).

Without acting lovingly it is of little value quoting various biblical texts that stress the love of God. Much of this is in fact religious cant, the proof of which is shown starkly by the unforgiving attitude of quite a few people who are 'very religious' in their outlook. They feel superior to the common mass who show no immediate interest in religion, and believe inwardly that they are closer to God because of their outer observance.

In fact, we are all equally close to God, who does not need any approval or invitation on our part to approach us. His nature is of such great love that he is the very basis of our life. The more we can be open to live in love and give of ourselves to our fellow creatures, the more aware do we become of the Divine source, and our consciousness deepens accordingly. In other words, the knowledge of God is one of receptivity; the more we try, the more certainly do we block that knowledge. On the other hand, the more spontaneous we are in our attitudes to our fellow creatures, the more open we are moment by moment to their Divine source. It is at that moment when religious practice can indeed move from mere ritual, and reveal something of a living touch inspiring it. When one worships God, self and all that appertains to it should have been swallowed up in a sea of ignorance. 'Unless you turn around and become like children, you will never enter the Kingdom of Heaven', said Jesus (Matthew 18:3).

Paradoxically, only those who are great of heart and inner intelligence can know the deeper meaning of this statement. Intelligence on a lower level commands everything for itself, and God too is swallowed up in that personal greed. Needless to say, God is not really swallowed up at all, but our 'knowledge' of God is now able to scintillate as spectacular ignorance. We therefore come to the surprising conclusion that assured professing religionists may often be further away from Divine reality than the humbler seeker who feels scarcely able to raise their eyes to the 'mighty ones' (in terms comparable to the parable of the Pharisee and the tax-collector which we have already considered).

The value of religion lies in setting the observant person in the right direction to a proper way of life; the universal injunctions of religion regarding faith, hope and love as well as the practice of moderation in all things and a concern for the well-being of other people as well as oneself are clearly guides to a way of life that leads to personal fulfilment, abundance and happiness, and also radiant communal relationships. Unfortunately these injunctions are usually followed only after one has been severely wounded and brought low in the process. Suffering remains our most important spiritual teacher, but this truth usually comes to us late in life. We feel that we ought to have had a better deal, and even are somewhat inwardly exultant when we hear of a famous individual suddenly brought low following a personal misfortune. This is one of the least attractive traits of human nature; it comforts us in tending to free us from the implied guilt of failure in some work that we ourselves had tried to execute. This malicious enjoyment of the misfortunes of other people is called *Schadenfreude*.

As a boy I was a loosely practising Jew, and although subsequently I moved closer and closer to Christianity I have never forgotten my own barmitzvah. First of all it occurred in 1940 just when the German army had invaded France, the Low Countries, Denmark and Norway, and a Nazi victory seemed inevitable, but even more important was the service itself. In the Reformed Synagogue the portion of the Law read by the boy is written in Hebrew but the portion of the Prophets is read in English. The portions used in my barmitzvah were Deuteronomy 5:6–21 and Jeremiah 31:31–4.

It gives me pleasure to quote this passage from Jeremiah:

> The days are coming, says the Lord, when I shall establish a new covenant with the people of Israel and Judah. It will not be like the covenant I made with their forefathers when I took them by the hand to lead them out of Egypt, a covenant they broke, though I was patient with them, says the Lord. For this is the covenant I shall establish with the Israelites after those days, says the Lord: I shall set my law within them, writing it on their hearts; I shall be their God, and they will be my people. No longer need they teach one another, neighbour or brother, to know the Lord; all of them, high and low alike, will know me, says the Lord, for I shall forgive their wrongdoing, and their sin I shall call to mind no more.

The Power of Creative Silence

To Mercy, Pity, Peace, and Love,
All pray in their distress:
And to these virtues of delight
Return their thankfulness.

For Mercy, Pity, Peace, and Love
Is God, our Father dear,
And Mercy, Pity, Peace, and Love
Is man, His child and care.

For Mercy has a human heart,
Pity a human face,
And Love, the human form divine,
And Peace, the human dress.

Then every man, of every clime,
That prays in his distress,
Prays to the human form divine
Love, Mercy, Pity, Peace.

And all must love the human form,
In heathen, Turk or Jew.
Where Mercy, Love & Pity dwell,
There God is dwelling too.

(William Blake, *Songs of Innocence*)

The principal use of religion lies in the practice of prayer. One can certainly pray devoutly without subscribing to any faith or attending any place of worship regularly. But without the discipline of regular worship inculcated by a religious tradition, an intention to pray regularly tends to become rapidly marginalized by worldly interests. Prayer is the heart of worship, and the validity of a religious tradition can be assessed by the strength and constancy of its worshippers. This activity is carried out in the silence of devoted contemplation. The juxtaposition of activity and silence appears on the surface to be contradictory, but in fact the soul is most active when we are still and attentive, for then its communication is direct and uncontaminated by intrusive thoughts.

How does one attain the silence which is the very heart of prayer? The number of techniques available are legion – their very number is an indication both of their necessity and their variable efficacy. In my experience, the way to silence is by a gradual dropping-off of thought by immersing oneself in a transparent sea of gratitude for the privilege of being alive at the present moment, and registering that moment as an event in its own right. In this silence the dross of worldly life is gradually cast off, and a vibrant freshness cleanses the soul of all clinging emotional desire. At last one can see clearly and discern the truth which liberates one from the usual bondage to material concerns. This truth illuminates the essence that underlies the appearances which dominate all our vision in worldly life. Indeed, we usually try to escape the impact of reality by retreating into a private world of specious illusion in which we can embellish our personal desires with flourishes of imagination. This mechanism releases us at least temporarily from many of the hard facts of life into a world of irresponsibility that can subside insidiously into futility.

True silence is very different: it releases us from the illusion of a private world into a knowledge of God's presence, which embraces the Divine love and recognizes nothing outside its care, no matter how aberrant its behaviour may be. On the contrary, the love of God enfolds all creation, which it elevates beyond mortality to an intimate reunion with itself and all its fellows. This is the basis of Divine forgiveness, which is the intimation of God's eternal care for his creatures. 'Let be then; learn that I am God.' ('Be still then, and know that I am God' is a well-known translation of Psalm 46:10 in the Authorised Version of the Bible.) This stillness is the way of our authentic knowledge of God's presence and his love. When one knows true silence, one brings others into its orbit also. In the end, one becomes a focus of silence that may, in a small way, have repercussions far beyond one's own cognizance. The distinctive feature of silence is its capacity to allow inner reflection. This is the basis of meditation, the result of which is the provision of time to reflect before one is tempted to do or say something unwise. It is unfortunate that the practice of most religions leaves little time for silence; religious observance frequently ends in loud conversation (and not to God primarily) with an element of controversy to enliven proceedings. When silence is lifted up to God in petition or intercession for oneself or for others, it moves into prayer.

The other uses of religion are less positive; their aim is admirable, but the human element cannot help but corrupt the good intention. It is a sad reflection on the human mind, but the two interests that cannot but carry the seeds of corruption within them are religion and politics. In respect of politics, despite the stirring ideals which flow profusely from party manifestos, in practice they all constantly betray the electorate that votes them into power. But only a very naïve person would expect otherwise, considering human moral weakness and the barely resistible corrupting power of worldly success, even in an especially responsible area of public service like politics. The same is unfortunately true of religion; illuminated as it may be by the witness of its saints, it is encompassed much more intimately by hypocrisy and prejudice among the congregation as well as the clergy. It is no surprise that many churches are dismally empty except when an internationally known, charismatic figure steals the limelight and draws thousands (or even millions), but after their departure the number of worshippers recedes to the usual low level. And yet the general interest in spiritual matters is at least as strong as ever. Spirituality unfortunately bears little constant relationship to religion. This tends to manipulate the concept of God to the use and convenience of humanity, but all too often is devoid of all concern, apart from the worshipper himself (and also the clergy).

I often wonder about the future of religion. It is evident that humanity has, as Dietrich Bonhoeffer said, 'come of age', but this maturation is intellectual rather than spiritual. Spiritually, we seem to be as childish now as we were before the advent of the great world religions. The proof of this provocative statement lies eloquently before us in the terrible things that Christians themselves have done, both to those outside their faith and also by those who believe that they alone follow the full way of Christ. To worship is the way to the good life rather than actually living it. This is the meaning of spirituality as opposed to religion. Humanity's mental tendency is one of conceptualization, but it is all too easy to turn a living being into a manipulable concept. It is evident that if religion is to play a positive role in the development of humanity it will need a total reappraisal of its limited end on earth.

The one certainty of life is its finite nature; this is God's greatest gift to life itself, otherwise we would have destroyed it after our own fashion. But if only we could learn to value each moment as it comes, as an event in its own right, we might then begin to value everything associated with that moment, especially our fellow human beings with whom we are obliged to live and work during our own short stay in this particular incarnation. If religion could help us to achieve this vital end, it would prove of immeasurable value. It has no justification apart from helping us to live the proper life; unfortunately, most people have a morbid loyalty to a form of religion which subtly assumes the nature of God. It is for this reason that one has sadly to admit that religion has at least as many abuses as uses to its credit, as each religion claims to be the repository of the absolute truth. One hopes that the present trend towards fundamentalism will be succeeded by a more open view to that which transcends all human understanding.

Communication by silence

During the days of my active ministry I conducted up to twelve retreats a year, and these were a very popular part of my work. A retreat may be thought of as a period when one moves away from the noise and clamour of everyday life and enters a place of peace, where silence is the most important element. In this silence one may begin to view aspects of oneself of which one was previously ignorant; this ignorance may not necessarily have been due to stupidity, but rather the result of having one's mind filled completely with worldly affairs. When the world is too much with us, it quite literally swallows us up, and our minds and lives are dominated by our relationships with those close to us, the daily round as well as political affairs, and the state of the world in general. 'To get away from it all' for even a few days can be a wonderful way of release, but only when our attention is focused on something very different. If we are accomplished in the use of silence, the practice that I mentioned previously will be more than adequate for us, but few could bear to be on their own for more than a very short period. The silence of a retreat is shared, and therefore is not unsociable in intention; on the contrary, such a shared silence can be closer to communion than the spoken word, which often by its very content can be divisive as easily as uniting. We know reality best when we are quiet and can listen, but paradoxically listening too intently can block the silence. It amounts to giving the ego full play and becoming progressively immersed in one's own interests and concerns. Therefore, the first requirement of a retreat is confidence with relaxation. Only then can one blossom inwardly (and outwardly also) and face the other retreatants with genuine affection. If the retreat continues for some length of time, one may begin to appreciate the presence of certain people to whom at the beginning one might have taken an instinctive dislike.

To be an effective conductor of retreats one has to be confident of one's own ability, and also be able to love people. An ideal retreat is not primarily about teaching; it is an adventure in getting to know a considerable range of people with the inner assurance that understanding and even love will be the end result. It is obvious therefore that the best retreat conductor is one with a considerable amount of self-knowledge, and this in my experience always requires prior suffering and disillusion. It is quite impossible to be an authentic spiritual teacher and healer while one is ignorant of the wounding edge of life and its complications. When one does have this knowledge and if one is the type of person I have already described, sympathy and affection spontaneously flow from one, and one cannot avoid being a support and teacher to the many unfortunate people looking for help. In other words, good retreat conductors are born rather than made. I do not believe that one learns how to conduct a retreat simply by attending courses on the subject; the only authentic teacher is one's own life, and since most people function mainly on an unconscious level, it is hardly surprising that they may end their lives as ignorant of basic reality as they were at the height of their powers. The same is unfortunately true of some ministers of religion. This is why organized worship tends to attract a steadily diminishing number of people.

From all this it appears that one should come on retreat with a clear mind completely open to new possibilities, yet at the same time alert to one's own need and humble enough to receive new information once one has accepted the authority of the conductor. This authority is a divine capacity, and this is why it cannot be prepared merely by intellectual development on its own. I started my retreat conducting life quite literally out of the blue; I was asked almost at the last moment to do something along this line, and I found that all that was required of me was to describe my own pertinent experience of life. I did not quote anything other than a few well-known biblical passages, and on looking back I can see that even these were there more to support my position as leader of the retreat than to enlighten any of the retreatants. As one becomes more of an authority in one's own right, so the need for outer justification becomes less essential. Through my years of retreat conducting, I certainly have become more knowledgeable on a wide range of subjects including theology, comparative religion, philosophy and psychology. The net conclusion of all this knowledge was to confirm what I already knew, that the so-called authority receives shafts of inspiration from on high which, if they are articulate, they can impart to lesser people. But in everyday life they are essentially ordinary, and subject to the same difficulties as other people. I often wonder how the great founders of religion appeared to their contemporaries. If one considers Jesus' disciples, one can see glaring faults in all their characters, yet they obviously had something that enabled them to transmit the message far beyond their own capacity to incorporate it immediately.

When I go on retreat in the capacity of conductor, I relax and smile. This is no artificial gesture, but rather an outer indication of the inner joy and expectancy of what lies ahead of me. I nearly always recognize a few faces, but even those who are new to me fill me with pleasant anticipation. I enter into the silence of prayer which I have described earlier, and at once a different type of consciousness envelops me. I can now speak confidentially to each person, which on the surface is quite absurd because confidential conversation must be individual, yet when the Holy Spirit is in charge, he speaks to each individual according to what that person needs to receive. I have time and time again been told by retreatants and church congregations that I have said exactly what they needed to hear. This again stresses the power of the Holy Spirit, for I certainly did not know the inner needs of even one person, let alone a considerable group of them.

I never cease to be amazed at the inner transformation that I can sense in various individuals who have come to a retreat that I have conducted – and presumably that other conductors have also led, for I would not wish to be classed as a person especially gifted in any spiritual sense. The basis of my retreats is getting up at about 7 a.m. which is either followed by the Eucharist or else breakfast, then the first address at about 10 a.m. The Eucharist would be at about 12 noon if it had not been celebrated earlier on. Lunch is at about 1 p.m. followed by a free period until the second address at about 5 p.m. with a tea interval for those who want it an hour before the second address. After the second address the time is entirely open to the retreatants' requirements, apart from supper which we have together. During the free periods I have special times available for individual consultation, but if possible I prefer the early afternoon period to be quiet for me also. No one can work spiritually 24 hours a day and survive long on such a rigorous mental regime. Supper is at about 7 p.m. and there is a session of communal prayer from 8 to 8.45 p.m. The day ends with Compline at about 9 p.m.

A retreat should be a period of enjoyment for everybody, not merely one of spiritual uplift. I encourage people not to take notes if possible, but rather to let the message sink directly into their minds. Note-taking is an excellent way of letting matters remain on a superficial level. In most cases the notes are kept, but are clearly seldom read with any depth, let alone frequency. It gives one a feeling of work well done to have notes like these, but if their content does not sink into the very soul of the person they are a waste of time. I regard the periods of consultation as the heart of my retreat, for then the individual can lay bare their heart to me as a confidential friend. If, I hope, sufficient wisdom comes to me to give some indication of the way forward for them, the proof or otherwise of work well done is the state of mind of the retreatant at the end of the retreat. At some retreats the gratitude is overwhelming, but more often the response is lukewarm. People have to develop an understanding of the spiritual life before they can appreciate what they have received. This, incidentally, is not due to my 'words of wisdom', but rather the atmosphere of friendship in the house of retreat and the relaxation that complete silence induces.

Most of the retreatants that I know are middle-aged and lonely adults, and it is always rewarding when a distinctly young person joins the group; on the surface such a person should feel out of place but if the retreat is well conducted and successful, that individual merges into the general flow of life without any difficulty at all. In my experience, one should never attempt to lower one's standards in order to embrace various types of people; one should always be oneself in any surrounding and the other person can either accept or reject one. We cannot be friends with everyone, nor should we try. If we can be ourselves with as much integrity as possible, we have indeed done what God wants of us, and that integrity will flow out to all around us, whatever their religion, class or colour. This is, incidentally, the way to overcome prejudices of various types: do not try at all except to be fully yourself. If only we could do this unaffectedly we would at least be surrounded by a large group of well-wishers. If only our politics and worship could be carried out in a similar vein it might be that both government and religion would be progressively purged of hypocrisy and intolerance, and become instead vital forums for the public at large to meet and learn to know each other.

The spiritual way is one of conflict with the forces that govern the world. The concept of fighting is by no means inadequate provided one sees the end as reconciliation rather than merely defeat of those opposed to the light. I end by quoting a hymn by John Monsell:

Fight the good fight with all thy might,
  Christ is thy strength, and Christ thy right;
Lay hold on life, and it shall be
  Thy joy and crown eternally.

Run the straight race through God's good grace,
  Lift up thine eyes, and seek his face;
Life with its way before us lies,
  Christ is the path, and Christ the prize.

Cast care aside, upon thy Guide
  Lean, and his mercy will provide;
Lean, and the trusting soul shall prove
  Christ is its life, and Christ its love.

Faint not nor fear, his arms are near,
  He changeth not, and thou art dear;
Only believe, and thou shalt see
  That Christ is all in all to thee.
              (*Hymns of Love and Praise*, 'Fight of Faith')

8 Beauty as an approach to God

If one considers beauty on a universal level, one finds that it is vitally important for many people in as much as their thoughts are raised from the concerns of this world to the aspiration of the soul through which we know God. In other words, music and also the other arts (the visual arts, prose and poetry) form an essential ingredient of a mature civilization. We start to be civilized when we live comfortably in community with others, but this is only the beginning of a process which ends in the divinization of all humanity. In the Eastern Orthodox tradition the word deification is used quite deliberately for this process, and indeed this should be the end of real religion. What is there about music that lifts us up to a knowledge of the Divine? It enters the soul and makes us aware not only of the Divine nature that lies at the heart of all creation, but even more particularly of our own soul, which is often spoken of as the heart. It is interesting in this respect that Jesus' first commandment was to love God with all our heart, and soul and mind and strength (Mark 12:30). In this case, the heart would represent the emotional nature of the human, but otherwise I would identify it with the soul. Certainly a warm-hearted individual fills my soul with joy, and I can for some time afterwards fulfil my proper role in the situation in which I find myself.

Musical composition, of course, started long before the time of the four great Viennese masters (Hayden, Mozart, Beethoven and Schubert); one thinks particularly of Handel and J. S. Bach. Their style was quite different from those who followed them, but their work attained as great a perfection as any of the later masters. Every fugue of Bach is pure truth in artistic form as are also the great oratorios of Handel. The Romantic composers who followed them, especially Mendelssohn, Schumann and Brahms, carried on the tradition initiated by Beethoven and Schubert and filled the entire world with soul-enhancing music that no one with sensitivity could ignore. It is interesting that when I was younger I had little time for the music of Mendelssohn and Liszt, but the maturing wisdom that is a product of the ageing process has made me more humble. Now I can appreciate Schumann's description of Mendelssohn as the Mozart of his time – no longer is he merely glib and superficial as I once considered him. During that period I dismissed the music of Liszt as being shallow and extremely exhibitionistic, but once again I have found a depth there which was previously hidden from my understanding. Greatness, in other words, stands the test of time and it is those who dismiss it prematurely who have ultimately to admit their error and begin to learn new ways. I am at last beginning to appreciate the music of such modern composers as John Tavener, Igor Stravinsky, Carl Nielsen and Witold Lutoslawski, while Samuel Barber's beautiful *Adagio for Strings* has long been one of my favourites. I have always regretted my inability to play an instrument well when music has been the source of my greatest inspiration, but listening has not been in vain because that inspiration has manifested itself through creative writing.

Pictorial art is immediately closer to us than music. One can so easily be completely deaf to the greatest music, as are some highly intellectual people whom I know, but no one can ignore art, whether in painting or as sculpture, because of the immediate impact it has through the eyes on the whole personality. Many people, however, can recognize only the surface structure, which can be shown much more accurately in a photograph. What indeed has a fine picture to offer that cannot be seen much more directly in a photograph? The answer lies in the details of the person or scene which has been depicted by the artist. The picture or sculpture has its own life which makes it a unique representation of the individual or scene at the present moment. Indeed, the painter or sculptor is as much present in the work as the person or object depicted. When one considers this in terms of art and music it is interesting to see how very unpleasant some extremely gifted artists and composers have been in real life. An obvious example is Richard Wagner, arguably the greatest of all operatic composers, whose virulent anti-Semitism formed an important link in uniting the German people to the racist theories of Nazism. Yet only a very bigoted listener could want to ignore Wagner's incomparable music.

In the realm of painting, Paul Gauguin was also unpleasant, being proud and ambitious. His behaviour towards Vincent Van Gogh, already mentally unbalanced, when they shared lodgings in Arles in southern France precipitated his suicide. Gauguin fled to Paris and two years later departed to Tahiti. In fact, the genius of an artist is not marred by their personal character; in other words, one does not need to be 'good' in order to be a great writer, artist or composer. The ways of genius are indeed strange, and if we are wise we are bound to be grateful for their contribution to civilization, sympathizing with rather than decrying their personal weaknesses. They have done enough in their life, short as it often is, to have justified their existence, and we should be indebted rather than judgemental in assessing their contribution to those who follow them.

The history of art is particularly interesting. I am a great admirer of the Italians, starting with Giotto and continuing with Fra Angelico, Mantegna, Botticelli, Leonardo da Vinci, Michelangelo, Raphael and the Venetian masters. Indeed, if one were to mention all the great Italian painters of the Renaissance, one could end up with a catalogue of names rather than a description of achievements, but their work was above all else an enormous tribute to the creative imagination of the human mind, when it concentrates on a particular theme which moves away from the usual desires of wealth, power and lust. I am, of course, not suggesting that any of these creative artists were saints and devoid of the usual human passions – indeed, they probably could not have done their work without the stimulus that these passions induced – but transcending the various worldly diversions to which we are all heir, they also worked in their superb creative magnificence. Neither music nor pictorial art can be of the slightest practical use to anybody except in inducing religious awe, national grandeur or political aspiration. When one thinks of art in this capacity it is only too easy to see how it may go amiss, inciting feelings of racial superiority or hatred as easily as lifting one up to something of the nature of God, which is always love. Indeed, art is the great means of communication of intangible truths, and those few people who have been richly endowed with this gift are bound to use it constructively for the benefit of others, for otherwise it can lead to incalculably severe destruction.

The art that particularly moves me is that of the Dutch seventeenth-century masters, especially Vermeer and Rembrandt. They have portrayed the human situation in a more perfectly intimate style than any other artists of whom I am aware. Their gift lies in working amongst the common people and portraying their everyday occupation in the same sort of way that one could imagine Jesus doing in the company of his disciples. It is, in my opinion, a far greater work to paint a very ordinary person, if not one who is frankly deformed, than a king in all his panoply. A painter who was able to portray royalty in a distinctly derisive vein was Francisco Goya, who worked at the end of the eighteenth century and whose portrait of the Spanish royal family played its own subversive part in fomenting the unrest of the French Revolution; art, as we see, transcends national barriers and belongs to all people. The English school of the eighteenth and early nineteenth centuries included the portraitist Gainsborough and the landscape painters Turner and Constable, while William Blake, the mystical writer and artist, brought his unique insights to public view.

Then we have to consider the French Impressionists at the

end of the nineteenth century and the beginning of the twentieth, including such artists as Manet, Degas, Renoir and Monet who were in turn succeeded by Cézanne, Seurat, Van Gogh and Gauguin. There followed Cubism, Expressionism and a new appreciation of the art of 'primitive people'. The end is Modernism. The deeper message of Impressionism was the capacity to portray a vista with individuals, whether human, animal or plant, as mere aspects of a much larger scene of light and colour. Few people could possibly view this vast cavalcade of painting with unanimous agreement, for we all have our own especial favourites, but as one grows in experience, as part of the ageing process, so one can begin to appreciate aspects of art that were previously hidden from one's gaze. The same is true of sculpture, which has the great advantage of producing a three-dimensional likeness of the subject that is portrayed. I especially revere the works of great painters and sculptors, like Bernini and Rodin, myself sadly lacking even the elements of creativity on this level. It is therefore not impossible for someone completely lacking in an artistic gift still to honour its practitioners.

The third great art form is literature, both in prose and in poetry. I think of the beginning of St Luke's Gospel, addressed to Theophilus:

> Many writers have undertaken to draw up an account of the events that had taken place among us, following the traditions handed down to us by the original eyewitnesses and servants of the gospel. So I in my turn, as one who has investigated the whole course of these events in detail, have decided to write an orderly narrative for you, your excellency, so as to give you authentic knowledge about the matters of which you have been informed.
>
> (Luke 1:1–4)

Indeed, in my opinion, the Bible stands far above any other single piece of literature, apart from its unique spiritual value. In many respects, the Old Testament is a better depiction of the human condition than the New Testament, largely because it is more down to earth and not afraid to recount disgraceful Israelite events as fully as those which are edifying.

The beauty of the Old Testament lies, as does Judaism for that matter, in its intense practicality and honesty. Sometimes it is horrifying in its brutality, but then so is so much of the history of humanity. When I come to the greatest of the writing prophets, Jeremiah, I can still hardly staunch the tears of ecstasy that come to my eyes. The whole of the subsequent Christian message, as well as humanity itself, is prophesied in the writings of the major prophets of the Old Testament. There is also the wonderful Wisdom Literature encapsulated particularly in the books of Job, Proverbs and Ecclesiastes that have a timeless quality of perfection about them, as well as being uncannily accurate in their assessment of the human condition: its inadequacy as well as its bravery under the most intolerable suffering. This is why I could never be anything other than a Christian with strongly Jewish roots.

The paradox of all this, of course, is the manner of Jesus' death after being rejected by his fellow Jewish contemporaries. But this again is the paradox of human nature. When something really beautiful appears it has in due course to be killed. Oscar Wilde has memorably expressed this in a passage from *The Ballad of Reading Gaol*:

> Yet each man kills the thing he loves,
> By each let this be heard,
> Some do it with a bitter look,
> Some with a flattering word.
> The coward does it with a kiss,
> The brave man with a sword!
>
> (Part 1, 7)

In respect of more secular prose I rank the novels of Dickens, Thackeray and Jane Austen particularly highly, to which I would add the novels of Tolstoy and Dostoievsky. All of these writers portray the human situation admirably. The writings of Victor Hugo have always been favourites of mine, and on the sociological level I would place the writing of Emile Zola on the highest rank.

Poetry is inherently more difficult to judge since our preferences are so individual. I personally rank the poetry of William Blake particularly highly because of its purity of vision and its inherent mysticism. One of his most beautiful poems is 'The Lamb':

> Little Lamb, who made thee?
> Dost thou know who made thee?
> Gave thee life, and bid thee feed,
> By the stream and o'er the mead;
> Gave thee clothing of delight,
> Softest clothing woolly bright;
> Gave thee such a tender voice;
> Making all the vales rejoice?
> Little Lamb? who made thee?
> Dost thou know who made thee?
>
> Little Lamb, I'll tell thee,
> Little Lamb, I'll tell thee;
> He is called by thy name,
> For he calls himself a Lamb.
> He is meek and he is mild;
> He became a little child.
> I a child and thou a lamb,
> We are called by his name.
> Little Lamb, God bless thee!
> Little Lamb, God bless thee!
> (*Songs of Innocence*)

What strikes one particularly is its absolute simplicity. It has no bravura or any striving for effect. Blake's mysticism is seen in a well-known quotation from *Auguries of Innocence*.

> To see a World in a Grain of Sand,
> And a Heaven in a Wild Flower,
> Hold Infinity in the palm of your hand
> And Eternity in an hour.

When one reads this excerpt one is immediately struck by an observation of Julian of Norwich,

Also in this He showed me a little thing, the quantity of an hazel-nut, in the palm of my hand; and it was as round as a ball. I looked thereupon with eye of my understanding, and thought: What may this be? And it was answered generally thus: It is all that is made. I marvelled how it might last, for methought it might suddenly have fallen to nought for little (littleness is what is meant). And I was answered in my understanding: It lasteth, and ever shall for that God loveth it. And so All-thing hath the Being by the love of God. In this Little Thing I saw three properties. The first is that God made it, the second is that God loveth it, the third that God keepeth it.

(Revelations of Divine Love, 5)

Another beautiful example of mystical poetry is the seventeenth-century poet Henry Vaughan's *The World* of which I quote the first stanza:

I saw Eternity the other night
Like a great ring of endless light,
   All calm, as it was bright;
And round beneath it, Time in hours, days, years
   Driven by the spheres
Like a vast shadow moved, in which the world
   And all her train were hurled.
The doting Lover in his quaintest strain
   Did there complain,
Near him, his lute, his fancy, and his slights,
   Wit's sour delights,
With gloves and knots, the silly snares of pleasure;
   Yet his dear treasure
All scatter'd lay, while he his eyes did pour
   Upon a flower.

My favourite quotation from William Wordsworth comes from his Ode 'Intimations of Immortality', from *Recollections of Early Childhood*. Here is the fourth stanza:

Our birth is but a sleep and a forgetting:
The Soul that rises with us, our life's Star,
   Hath had elsewhere its setting,
   And cometh from afar:
   Not in entire forgetfulness,

And not in utter nakedness,
But trailing clouds of glory do we come
 From God, who is our home:
Heaven lies about us in our infancy!
Shades of the prison-house begin to close
 Upon the growing Boy,
But he beholds the light, and whence it flows,
 He sees it in his joy;
The Youth, who daily farther from the east
 Must travel, still is Nature's priest,
 And by the vision splendid
 Is on his way attended;
At length the Man perceives it die away,
And fade into the light of common day.

This passage summarizes my view of eternity absolutely.

Natural beauty

It is all too easy to forget the beauty that surrounds us day
by day when we restrict ourselves only to the beauty that
has arisen from the human mind. Jesus in the Sermon on the
Mount reminds us not to be anxious about clothes but to
consider the lilies that grow in the fields; they do not work,
they do not spin; yet he reminds us that even Solomon in all
his splendour was not attired like one of them (Matthew
6:28–29).

As one moves from the bare vista of winter to the first
glimmerings of spring, so the welcome flowers make their
first appearance in the landscape. First there is the humble
snowdrop, which is soon followed by crocuses, daffodils,
narcissi and tulips; these are succeeded by the beautiful
blossoms that glorify many of our trees and then follow the
roses and the abundance of summer. This magnificent array
of beauty is so taken for granted by most of us that we begin
to appreciate its glory only when it starts to decline as the
days shorten and summer is succeeded by autumn. Even
then, the leaves, before their final death, show wonderful
russet tints, but all is finally brought low by the first frosts

of winter. Winter is always a depressing season, even if it is enlivened by various celebrations, including Christmas itself, and one looks in eager expectation for the panoply of spring. The succession of flowers is repeated year after year, but they never cease to re-awaken joy and gratitude in the eyes of all who have moved beyond self-centredness to participate in life on a more universal level.

Our animal brethren also have their particular beauty. We remember particularly William Blake's poem on the Tyger (from *Songs of Experience*). The point of that famous poem is that God is the creator of all things, ruthless and terrible as well as glorious and life affirming. This indeed is the mystery of life, that evil is a part of creation and will never be removed simply by human brilliance. The way forward, as I see it, is one of tenderness and care so that we may affirm that nothing that lives is foreign to us. At present we aim to assert this only with regard to our fellow human beings, but this is no longer adequate when we see that all that lives is part of an enormous ecosystem. It is indeed difficult to include frankly noxious organisms, plants and animals in this scheme, and here we have to admit our ignorance in the face of a mystery. When human beings take control, they are much more likely to destroy the beauties of nature for the benefit of modern technology; it could well be that the ugliest of all creatures is none other than humans themselves.

A passage from the seventeenth-century mystical writer Thomas Traherne embraces the mysticism of natural beauty,

> You never enjoy the world aright, till you see how a sand exhibiteth the power and wisdom of God: and prize in every-thing the service which they do you, by manifesting his glory and goodness to your Soul, far more than the visible beauty on their surface, or the material services they can do your body.
>
> You never enjoy the world aright, till the Sea itself floweth in your veins, till you are clothed with the heavens, and crowned with the stars: and perceive yourself to be the sole heir of the whole world, and more than so, because men are in it who are

every one sole heirs as well as you. Till you can sing and rejoice and delight in God, as misers do in gold, and Kings in sceptres, you never enjoy the world.

(*Centuries of Meditation* 1, 27 and 29)

9 Freedom:
the eternal quest

Freedom is something that all rational people desire. It also is among the most misused concepts in history. If people were asked what would really make them free, they would mention some of the qualities already discussed in previous chapters, such as wealth, power, love, and above all the capacity to direct their own lives according to their own will. Yet the paradox remains: the more of these qualities one has, the less satisfied one is with one's present lot. I mentioned right at the beginning the futility of great wealth; the one thing it does not appear to provide is inner security and the same would apply to power, relationships with other people and even our own health. The reason for this apparent paradox is that these qualities, while by no means to be disparaged, all tend to drive one more and more into one's own personality. If I, for instance, desired to become really renowned, all other considerations in life would be subjected to this one driving passion and I would not be free to develop other sides of my own nature. Indeed, in a interesting way, passion is the reverse side of the coin of freedom; without passion one cannot live properly as a unique individual, but without freedom one's passion becomes the ruling theme of one's existence. The one way in which the paradox can be resolved is by accepting it, giving it due recognition in one's life and moving far beyond its scope; only then can one see that true freedom is attained by devoting one's life selflessly to the world at large.

All this is, needless to say, much more easily said than done, and only when one has undergone a shattering experience, such as I described in the first chapter, and many more have undergone in our terrible century of genocide, if one has been fortunate enough to emerge alive; only then, I say, can one glimpse the real meaning of freedom. Some of the Bible brings this idea into close focus. The story of Job is typical: only when he has come to terms with the loss of everything can he start to become a real person. At the end of the narrative, though all his material possessions including a new family are restored, he is now a much calmer man and able to take life as it comes, without trying to placate anybody, even God himself. It seems strange that religion can alienate one from God quite as easily as bringing one closer to a relationship with him. The more we try, the more certain it is that we will fail. On a material level this is obviously nonsense as I am learning even with my unceasing endeavours to walk better than I do at the moment, yet on a spiritual level a rather different law is at work.

The reason for this is not difficult to understand: what one strives for on a material level is quite clearly egoistical, no matter how convincingly it may be presented in terms of the common good, for there is no doubt that it is very elevating to be highly regarded by other people, and the more one denies this, the more one deceives oneself. On a purely personal level we all look for some sort of reward. It is quite possible that no work would be done at all if there were not some personal motive or reward attached to the end of it. Of course we need adequate wages in order to survive, and few of us would care to live at subsistence level if we had the choice. On the other hand, an increase in income is the spur to greater work, so that we may acquire more substance and achieve greater influence in our society until the final judge, Death, comes to close the scene and show us in our naked reality how very insignificant we are as individuals. I find it extremely entertaining to watch the news on television and see the currently influential personalities parading themselves in speech and form before my gaze as I eat my evening meal; how revealing their startling naïvety is! They are here today and gone tomorrow, as is the case also of 'celebrities' who capture the public imagination for a month or so and then disappear, only to be replaced by some new sensation. How right Jesus was when he told his disciples to beware of those who spoke well of them, for so did their predecessors speak of the false prophets. We like to hear what boosts our ego but there is no freedom in this attitude, because we are completely subject to the opinions of other people and few of these are very stable.

In the Buddhist ethic detachment plays a vital role in the development of the person, yet we know that the very essence of communal life lies in attachment to other people. Without this there could be no stable union between man or woman, or even a strong friendship, yet attachment does limit one's freedom very considerably. To marry these two concepts is one of the great tests of a successful human life. In fact, if we consider the matter clearly we can see that attachment loses its dominating quality only when it becomes widely dispersed amongst an ever-increasing group of people whom we may legitimately call friends. When one sees attachment on this elevated level, it no longer demands anything for itself at all but is concerned for the whole. This starts on the level of an intimate group of people, but the end should be a concern and love for all humanity, indeed all life. The founders of the world's major religions show this to greater or lesser extent; I personally feel that Jesus and Gautama are the great exemplars.

There are two important limitations to freedom: impotence and licence. The impotent individual is completely in bondage to those who are more powerful. At one time this was the social position of many women, but now fortunately this role has disappeared: in fact, throughout all generations many women have had the upper hand through their emotional power, and many men, despite their physical strength, have been emotionally dependent. One can therefore only begin to understand freedom as one grows into greater identity. This identity starts on a personal level, but when one approaches the realm of mysticism one knows the ultimate identity ever more intimately. I am speaking quite

clearly of the Divine Nature. In such a situation all one's
fellow humans are brethren, and any desire for power is
lifted up towards a movement of freeing all subject people
to actualize their own unique identity. I would go so far as
to say that the person who throws their weight around is in
fact also demonstrating their inherent weakness. If I, for
instance, wrote to show my superlative knowledge in some
subject, anyone with experience and a sense of humour
would see through my brilliance in a trice to a weak person
who needed to display themself in all their finery in order to
impress their fellow creatures. One thinks again of the
television personalities who play such an interesting part in
our entertainment day by day.

Those who are licentious are in fact the slaves of their
own desires. A classical example is Don Juan himself; his
passion for all types of women was so extreme that he could
only realize himself in the act of seduction. Mozart shows
this particularly well in *Don Giovanni*. At present many
members of the younger generation have moved from com-
mendable freedom to irresponsible licence. We discussed this
in Chapter 6 in relation to sexual relationship outside marriage. But licentiousness can also involve political power,
wealth, alcohol and drugs of various types. In these examples
the person is so free that they have betrayed their individual
liberty by being addicted to one comparatively small element
of life.

What, then, is the way to a fuller understanding of freedom? It is, indeed, as has been spelled out so frequently in
these pages, the way of self-transcendence. As long as we are
the basis of our consciousness and our desires are our sole
way of life, we can never move beyond the ego. While we
are trapped in egoism we cannot be free, even if we have
everything material that the heart could desire. This thought
has been pointed out to us on more than one occasion in the
teachings of Jesus – the rich young man was told to forfeit
his wealth if he was to know true fulfilment. Then alone
could he enter into the company of the Master and his
disciples. As we have already noted, this change of heart

nearly always follows some crippling injury in which the things that one really values are simply removed from one as a result of misfortune. Sophocles (495–406 BC) said 'Call no man fortunate who is not dead, for the dead alone are free from pain'. He also said 'Not to be born is best' (*Oedipus at Colonus*). In this play Oedipus, the tragic king of Thebes who unwittingly killed his father and married his mother, finally finds release. The Buddha said that all life is suffering. He believed that suffering was due to desire and the way to overcome it was to transcend personal desire. All this is extremely illuminating and depressing; it is doubtful whether any human being acts according to this excellent advice because if they did they would be denying their own identity also.

One of the many paradoxes of life is that in order to love one's neighbour one has first to love oneself; if there is no self-worth at all, it is difficult to envisage anyone recognizing the worth of anything else. It is fortunate that the Buddhist also speaks of the Middle Way, though extremists, of course, will never practise it properly. In modern life the 'common man' has much greater freedom in acquiring material substance. The result has been far better public health and the dubious advantage of living on to the point of senility. As more cheerful observers would say, 'You can't win'. This seems to be the nature of life itself. One is bound to the prison of mortality as long as one is alive, yet no one other than the person in a state of severe depression desires death.

This fear of death is not simply a religious mirage based on the theme of a punitive God; it is part of the human condition, for in its wake is the fear of total extinction. It was this fear that was so categorically annulled in me following my momentous near-death experience, but I often wonder how many people would have survived the ordeal that I was destined to undergo. As I said previously, it produced a complete change in my way of looking at life. But unfortunately one still is encased in one's own particular environment and this precludes absolute freedom. We do not live for ourselves alone but for the whole world; without its aid we could not keep alive for more than a second.

Freedom on a political level implies that every citizen has the right to choose their own destiny as far as the workings of their country are concerned. How true this is in fact is much more questionable. Dictatorship is the complete reverse of freedom; I doubt whether anyone would deny this, but is its reverse, democracy, so much freer in the end? Our lives are conditioned moment by moment by the rules that govern our society. If we really were completely free, it is much more likely that we would lapse into a most destructive type of licentiousness, hence the law is a vital part of our civilization. The end of a constructive life lies in tailoring one's own particular gifts and efficiencies to the cloth of communal responsibility. This admirable advice is possible only when one has lost concern for oneself as a unique individual far more important than anyone else.

The aim of all real religion is to produce this liberated humility in its adherents, but in fact the brilliant understanding of the great founders of religion is soon used by the generation of disciples that follow simply to elevate themselves as the ones who know the full truth. An enlightened minority may admittedly have a more universal approach, but yet it is important to accept oneself as unique, for otherwise one will fail to do the particular task that has been allotted one in this particular lifetime. In the face of so much paradox it seems to me wise above all else to do the work of the present moment with as much perfection as is possible, remembering that every individual has their own uniqueness. When they set to work actualizing this tendency they move beyond self-concern to concern for the world at large. This, I believe, is the true way of freedom. It is obviously a counsel of perfection for we do tend to love ourselves very much in the ordinary state of life, and become depressed only when we fail to reach our particular goal. Hence the end of freedom is not self-abnegation so much as self-forgetfulness. Only when I know I am nothing, a knowledge made obvious by the limited duration of life I have on this earth, can I cease from thinking about myself and lapsing into vain imagination. Instead I will do the present work as perfectly as I can and let the day take care of itself. This is a vital teaching in the Sermon on the Mount (Matthew 6:34), and something similar can be found in the writings of all the great religious geniuses.

Life, because it seems so difficult, is actually our way of simplicity. Only when I know that I can do very little in the short spell of life ahead of me, even if I were a far younger person than I am, can I really get rooted in the present moment and all that appertains to it. When I know this even for a short period of time, I am completely free. This applies even to those who have great worldly responsibilities, including marriage and caring for the family. One of the great illusions of life, which never ceases to amuse me, is the alleged indispensability of some people. When the great name dies and suitable tributes are paid to it in all the leading newspapers, the personage is soon swallowed up in oblivion and the world continues very much as it did before this great event. As they say when the monarch dies and the successor is appointed. 'The King is dead, long live the King.' Indeed, the person may be dead but the affairs of the world progress steadily onwards. All this is in keeping with a theme of the Wisdom Literature of the Old Testament.

Futility, utter futility, says the Speaker,
everything is futile.
What does anyone profit from all his labour
and toil here under the sun?
Generations come and generations go,
while the earth endures for ever.

The sun rises and the sun goes down;
then it speeds to its place and rises there again.
The wind blows to the south,
it veers to the north;
round and round it goes and returns full circle.

All streams run to the sea,
yet the sea never overflows;
back to the place from which the streams ran
they return to run again.

(*Ecclesiastes* 1:2–7)

The profound truth of this passage cannot be denied, though from time to time the workings of the world are disrupted by natural disasters such as earthquakes, floods and droughts. 'As it was in the beginning, is now, and ever shall be: world without end. Amen.' What does change in this endless cycle is the birth of a new soul into the world. Maybe the Messiah will be among us even now, coming in glory to judge the living and the dead as affirmed in the Nicene Creed.

The conditions for freedom

If a child was granted instant freedom, we all know what the result would be – disaster and even death. Therefore the primary requirement for freedom is responsibility. As I have mentioned on more than one occasion, this is not always a predominant factor in our present age. Freedom soon degenerates into licentiousness if strong barriers are not first imposed. It would be best if these were self-imposed, and indeed in the person moving towards fulfilment and happiness they would be so imposed, but the less civilized individual would at once take the law, as they see it, into their own hands. Once one is subject to the law, primarily personal law but also civil law, a remarkable freedom comes to one. Now one can really begin to feel safe, not only from the attacks of criminals but also, and far more important, from one's own unconscious drives which could land one in serious trouble. Here one thinks of addictions of various types and also sexual impropriety.

Freedom demands in addition a respect for the right and dignity of other people; these, then, in turn will tend to respect one and in so doing strengthen one's own freedom. This approach can be broadened to our concern for the environment. On one level it is here for our use and disposal, but if we continue to behave inconsiderately to it, it will shrivel up in front of our very noses, and we will be left to starve in consequence. Freedom should grant freedom to others under its care; thus parents should respect the individuality of their children. If this self-respect is granted, the child is much more likely to follow in the path set by the parent than they might otherwise have done. But, one always has to be careful to set limits to activities. In our quest for freedom we often walk the tightrope between licentiousness on the one hand, and strangulating obedience on the other. All this is very hard for we tend to know the answers beforehand, particularly when they appertain to other people. Therefore humility is a crucial factor in the proper exercise of freedom. Humility with restraint has to work hand in hand with a demand for obedience. If this works well the person (especially a child) will grow immensely as a result, and their ultimate gratitude will be very impressive.

The third chapter of this book dealt with power. Power both inhibits freedom and makes it possible, for without it the freedom would run amuck until the individual was overcome, even destroyed by someone with greater power. The end therefore of freedom properly applied is the growth of the person into a mature adult, in which state they can apply the laws of power and freedom independently. This is the ideal situation of government also, and if a democracy works on these lines – something I fear that is not so very common – the social health of the community will be assured.

In the history of humanity oppressive regimes have after a variable period been destroyed and replaced by governments selected by the people themselves. It is rather uncommon for this state to continue indefinitely, except in very advanced societies, as in most of Western Europe nowadays.

10 Truth and illusion

Truth can be seen on various levels. It is most satisfactory when it can be most directly proven; this is scientific proof, and it is constantly being expanded by new knowledge. But the truth that concerns us particularly as people is the validity of our belief system and above all our inner nature. It is obvious to me that the really important things of life cannot be proven in any way other than experience. When people try to bring religion and science together they nearly always distort the scientific view to suit themselves. The tangible cannot be easily connected to the intangible, yet it is by truth that has come to one on a very personal level that one in the end leads one's life.

What, for instance, is the truth about myself? On a personal level, I would have to admit remarkably little, although I am now an elderly man. Even my appearance, as I see in photographs, does not entirely match up to the face that confronts me day by day as I shave it. When I compare myself pictorially with what I was twenty years ago, the difference is even more marked. By this simple example one can see that although truth does not change, the subject of it is undergoing constant remodelling. But what concerns me particularly in relationship to happiness is our inner attitude. In the end, it matters little what you think about me externally, whether I am handsome or ugly, for instance, but what you feel about my character and therefore my integrity is quite a different matter. Most of us take life seriously, aim at least to be decent, law-abiding citizens, and if we are 'religious' we would want to be perfect in the way that Jesus counselled his disciples. He said 'There must be no limit to your goodness, as your Heavenly Father's goodness knows no bounds' (Matthew 5:48). In the Authorised Version of the Bible this is expressed more compellingly as, 'Be ye perfect as your Father in Heaven is perfect'.

This counsel on a purely practical level, the so-called counsel of perfection, in fact is, I have no doubt, beyond the capability of even the most sincere person. Furthermore, there is even a place for lying according to the circumstances. Behaviour cannot be reduced to simple rules. This surely must make the eyebrows rise, but if I were, for instance, to ask you for your opinion about something I had written and you really disliked it, common politeness should lead you to temper your criticism and even to damn it with faint praise, if you felt particularly concerned for my feelings. The same approach might apply to your comments about my appearance, accent or antecedents. It would be cruel if you told me what you actually thought about any of these things, because you might diminish me to the extent of my being completely crushed. If I had a tendency to depression, I might even contemplate suicide. The compassion that guides a softening down of unpleasant necessity is called tact or 'sugaring the pill'. One is wise to sugar the pill of criticism of another person's creative work.

Likewise, would it be such a terrible crime to steal a loaf of bread to feed a destitute individual, if you yourself had none available at that time? Of course, I would expect you to replace the money for the bread subsequently, as the Good Samaritan promised to do when the man who had fallen among thieves and been half killed was sent by him after emergency treatment to an inn (Luke 10:30–37). Therefore, even if one were to perform an action which was obviously deviant, the reason should be valid and the repayment prompt.

If we look critically at ourselves, how many illusions are we likely to find? If we are ordinary people, we will have little difficulty in detecting various weaknesses in our character and might even be rather light-hearted in our self-criticism. If, on the other hand, we aspired to holiness, we might see fewer defects and even become rather smug in our own assessment. We have considered this situation already in relation to the Pharisee and the tax-collector. I wonder why the tax-collector went home acquitted of his sins but not the self-righteous Pharisee (Luke 18:10–14). Like Job, but on a much cruder level, the Pharisee was full of pride; after all, his conduct and actions were irreproachable, but he was far too self-centred and showed little compassion for people who might have been 'less advanced' than he considered himself. Indeed, our universal illusion is self-opinionation. Even those who have an inbuilt low self-esteem are by no means exempt from this grave fault; they worship the image that they would like to have, had circumstances been different. If one leads the spiritual life in earnest the first lesson is always to accept oneself gratefully and let that gratitude flow out to all those around one, irrespective of their merit. Indeed, if one has fulfilled this challenge, one is well on the way to the perfection that Jesus demanded. How can we really be as perfect as God? This is surely ridiculous, until we remember the momentous statement of 1 John 4:7–8, 'Let us love one another, because the source of love is God. Everyone who loves is a child of God and knows God, but the unloving know nothing of God, for God is love.'

We cannot love either our neighbour or God until we love ourselves, and this love does not come easily to the conscientious person. That person may try to live a more admirable life and eventually become like the Pharisee. We know only too well where that can lead. Only when one has accepted oneself as one truly is, warts and all, can one begin to accept other people on their terms also – no longer merely with condescending toleration but instead with increasing affection. A person's particular mannerisms become rather lovable, even if one knows that some of their statements are not to be taken seriously. This is part of the commerce of daily living. As one accepts various peculiar people, so one begins to realize how peculiar one is oneself, if not in their particular way nevertheless in an equally strange way, and one's eyes begin to lighten. This is the beginning of one of the great gifts that we all have, but only some really know how to use properly a sense of humour.

Some people seem to have an innate sense of humour and their character seems to be sanguine or cheerful. Others have a natural tendency to gloom, suspicion, anger or jealousy. Some are fanatics – and here religion has more than its share; they do not laugh because they know the answer beforehand, even if that answer is self-destructive. It is very hard for this type of person to empathize closely with any person who does not share their own type of belief. It is on this level that religion and politics can become a dire menace, and persecutions as well as the more secular dictatorships find their origins. Consider, for instance, the most notorious exemplar of this in our own time, Adolf Hitler. Can you imagine him laughing? The answer is 'Yes, of course I can'. But at what would he be laughing? He would be deriding another person's discomfiture on racial or political grounds, and would be overjoyed if that unfortunate individual were to be killed. Therefore it is possible to obtain enjoyment in being fanatic or grossly intolerant, say, about matters sexually aberrant. But this is not a sense of humour; it is simply an enjoyment derived through witnessing another person's discomfiture. The basis of true humour, that at which everyone can laugh, is the juxtaposition of incongruous images. These are out of place or absurd, and the great comedies of literature and music have been based upon the contrast between a character and his pretensions.

Fanatics like Hitler have little sense of humour; it is replaced by a cruel depiction of those whom they despise and reject, even to the point of hatred. One can imagine a fanatic smiling with delight when his 'enemy' has been rejected or hurt, but there is no fun in his mirth. Humour can be cruel also as when one laughs spontaneously at a vain person's sudden discomfiture. But what I would call pure humour clears the mind, at least for a time, of any serious preoccupation; even if the joke is pure nonsense, it brings one back to sanity once more. The most fundamental and important type of humour consists in being able to view oneself dispassionately and laugh at one's own foibles. These are individual weaknesses of character on which one mistakenly prides onself. How easy it is to say 'I hate mean people or those who display racial prejudice', while concealing from one's own vision a weakness of character on which one unconsciously prides oneself. A person who really exhibited these standpoints would not need to proclaim them at all; they would simply act the part in everyday life so that no one had any illusions about their views.

A fine sense of humour lends balance to the personality, particularly if it is over-inflated or sadly dejected. One would not expect much of a sense of humour in those who are mentally ill. The paranoid individual would be dominated by a sense of persecution, whereas those of a cyclothymic temperament would veer between excesses of mania and depression. The maniac might appear to have a sense of humour, but they would be laughing at their own private joke which might be quite irrelevant to the event at hand and often decidedly cruel.

It follows, therefore, that a sense of humour is the means whereby illusions can be counteracted, and in due course they may be neutralized also. A bald statement of the truth, on the other hand, might merely stir up a person's illusions, and a vicious conflict might ensue. If only we did know the truth about ourselves, it would set us free as Jesus taught (John 8:32). In this particular chapter of John's Gospel it is proclaimed that the Son can alone free one to know the truth, therefore the consciousness of God is our only way to the ultimate truth about ourselves. Anything else is second-hand and questionable.

God, it seems, uses various ways to bring us to our senses and to truth. Job had to suffer absolute destitution before he learnt that he of himself was nothing apart from the Divine grace. In the case of lesser people who flatter themselves on their intellectual excellence, an awakening of their sense of humour may bring them down to earth, but this is unlikely to occur until they themselves have been brought low. Although many of the characters in the great comedies are obvious caricatures, they are also too near the truth about ourselves to be lightly dismissed. A person with an acute sense of humour delights in their own fallibility, indeed their own foibles, when they see them in a clear light. Such a person is capable of learning much about themselves and at the same time about other people and the world in general. The truth that is revered in John's Gospel is not merely scientific evidence, which is easy enough to demonstrate if one possesses the appropriate technique; it is the truth about life itself, which always concerns the individual primarily. When one is attuned to one's own being, one is automatically at peace with other people and can start to do one's work with a clear mind and a joyous heart. The evil of persistent illusions is that they obscure our real identity from our awareness. Whereas a delusion is a false impression or opinion, an illusion deceives the truth of a matter without contradicting it outright. The person who prides themself on racial tolerance, for instance, might genuinely aspire to this quality, but in fact their general attitude to 'foreign' people denies it time and time again.

From all this, it is apparent that, while objective scientific proof is easily within the compass of any suitably trained individual, the inner truth of our own personality comes only in slow stages to us. It is seldom apparent in children or even young adolescents; the inevitable reverses of life consequent on relationships make it more apparent to all of us, so that when we attain full adult stature we should have at least some awareness of our weaker characteristics. These are not to be disparaged, because they are our means of growth; when they are acknowledged quite frankly and acted upon, they may at the beginning tend to lead us astray, but experience ought to control them and ultimately marry them with our full character.

Thus if I disclaim a display of racism while harbouring it deep in my heart, the way forward is to accept it as an integral part of my character, while acknowledging its inadequacy. Then it will in the course of time become less obtrusive. This really means that one should love oneself in one's entirety and not in any way ignore those facets of one's character which one finds disagreeable. If one can achieve this end, one is well on the way to personal integrity, and a mature person will emerge from the experience. Therefore truth does not flinch from any experience or attitude, no matter how unpleasant or even criminal it may be. But if a person accepts it generously as part of his or her own character, it is gradually transfigured into something quite beautiful. I would much rather have unpleasant attitudes of this type and learn to cope generously with them, than be perfect as the Pharisee in the parable so obviously considered himself, to say nothing of poor old Job.

The end of our growth as individuals is to have fully rounded personalities, not so much good as genuine. This is called self-actualization. Religion has far too many 'good' people associated with it, and they tend above all else to alienate others on the path. Indeed, if one is genuinely on the path, one's deficiencies are unconsciously incorporated into one's character and one grows in empathy with all types of people. Such unpleasant tendencies as sexism, racism and class prejudice simply fall away as one realizes, as the Roman writer Terence (*c.* 190–159 BC) wrote: 'I am a man, I count nothing human indifferent to me' (*Heauton Timorumenos* 1.1.25). I find this particularly interesting because Terence would be classed as a pagan, yet nothing in the scriptures advances that view or denies it; it really is another form of the second commandment stated by Jesus, 'You must love your neighbour as yourself' (Leviticus 19:18; Matthew 19:19). It might be objected that the difficulty about commandments like those in the Sermon on the Mount is not so much their truth but their impracticability, if one reads them in one fell swoop. But I believe that if such teachings are inculcated with love into the minds of the young at a very early age they stick, and then form the basis of future actions. In other words, teaching should be actualized immediately.

It seems to me that truth on a moral level is universal in scope; the various world religions set their finest practices in daily living and do not merely preach it on suitable occasions. If this were the rule generally, there would be far fewer illusions in the minds of most people. Most illusions have a grandiose character, but some might have a diminishing effect. If we stopped thinking so much about ourselves, either positively or negatively, and instead proceeded steadily with the work at hand we would know the truth in the present moment. This is indeed the truth that sets one free from all illusions and other temptations also. It is on this level that religious education is in my opinion crucially important in the development of the character of young people. In connection with our general consideration of happiness, we will never know this most desirable state until we know ourselves as we really are and can accept that knowledge also. Only then do the various desires that have already been dealt with in previous chapters find their correct place in our lives. They cease to dominate, but are merely spurred on to greater satisfaction in the future.

This consideration of illusion must extend further than one's own personality; it should also include those whom we love, those with whom we work day by day, and also the idols that captivate audiences by the means of mass communication. One has only to see the faces of some of these people on television, for instance, to see the insecurity that lies behind the confident words that they utter. One is unlikely to be free of the illusion of seeing other people as particularly great until one knows oneself better. We after all have to be the yardstick by which other mortals are measured. I myself find that those who criticize on a large scale and those who exult in their own piety are particularly insecure people. It is so easy to cloak one's own deficiencies under an issue of words full of sincerity but in the end meaning very little. 'You will recognize them by their fruit', said Jesus (Matthew 7:20). When the fruit is sound not only is the tree flourishing, but also those who partake of it are nourished. This is the test whereby truth can be distinguished from illusion; it simply does not fill one with joy but rather leaves one peculiarly empty. I suppose at an early period of our life our illusions may be stepping stones towards truth, but in due course it is right that they be left behind as we move ever onward to the true peak of truth. When we have attained this we can really understand and obey the scriptures, and move some distance towards attaining their precepts also.

Attitudes

Our attitude is the way in which we confront the various circumstances of our life day by day; it is our settled way of behaviour as indicating our opinion. There is both the specific attitude related to a particular event and also a more general attitude that typifies our response to the various ingredients of life itself. Our attitude of mind is indeed our settled mode of thinking. Children's attitudes are determined essentially by the nature of the circumstances surrounding them; for instance, there is the time when events satisfy the child and then they behave well, bringing with them warm affection. On the other hand, a deleterious turn of events soon changes this glowing attitude to life, and the child will rapidly become obstinate and unco-operative. If the child is not allowed to express themself freely, they will learn to conceal their true feelings, and their motive will become distorted and their character warped and unsociable. On the other hand, too much latitude allows gross distortions of acceptable attitudes to manifest themselves. The old adage, 'Spare the rod and spoil the child', now distinctly unpopular to put it mildly, has ageless wisdom. It seems that one needs to have attained considerable maturity from experience before one is truly civilized; this is an attitude of deep concern for individuals apart from oneself and ultimately society in general.

The cult of the individual and personal greed which typified the 1980s has brought its reward in society, and I therefore would welcome an attitude of far greater individual and social responsibility. The millennium is upon us, and it would be encouraging if this were heralded not so much by the reappearance of the Messiah as by a radical change in heart and mind of all people so that they could assume adult responsibility with genuine rejoicing. This could be the new messianism.

Integrity

One's character is formed as one approaches adult life – it may be straight and honest or crooked and devious. More likely, there will be a mixture of these extremes, tailored to suit the situation. It seems to me that character traits are both inherent and acquired. By this I mean that we bring with us certain attitudes that are as much part of our identity as any of our bodily features, but unlike these physical elements our character is constantly being moulded and reshaped during childhood and to a lesser extent in adolescence also.

I have known several instances of two siblings of the same sex with polar opposite characters; one has been cheerful and outgoing whereas the other remained taciturn and suspicious. The parents of this type of family have been remarkably kind, considerate people whom I have liked immensely, and I have always wondered how it is that two children from the same environment should be so totally different. I have not in any way disliked either child, but cannot help seeing how assiduously the unfriendly one builds up a mounting wall of isolation around himself or herself. If they marry, a separation is almost inevitable, and the partner is always blamed for the break-up. I feel on balance that we are individuals from the moment of our conception, and subsequent influences work on a prior foundation. What therefore is one to do if one is lumbered with a negative type of personality? If one is aware of the situation, one has to learn to accept it unflinchingly and do all one can to give of oneself to other people, no matter how low one's own self-esteem may be. To a limited extent I have experienced this unfortunate tendency, but having mastered it through a combination of Divine grace, a strong power of will and complete honesty, I have made something of my life. It has never been easy, but, thank God, I have something to show for it in terms of productivity and the help it is claimed that I have given to others in the fields of counselling and healing. If one can accept the situation with the same truth as one could if afflicted by a congenital defect of sight, hearing or posture, one can aim at the possible, and then to one's amazement impossible things may start to happen. Now I no longer feel inferior to anybody, realizing that we all have our own cross to bear, and those who are brave enough to confront it early on have the best opportunity of making something really valuable of their lives. What I am saying is in effect that happiness of a durable type is achieved after braving a dark journey bordering sometimes almost on despair. Yet, pressing onwards with an almost supernatural strength based on hope, one is, in the process, learning something of life's inner secret.

Integrity is defined as wholeness or soundness when applied to an article, but in terms of personality it depicts uprightness and honesty. It demands complete acknowledgement of who and what one is, and if one is earnest in one's toil, one will see looming distantly in front of one's inner gaze a host of unfavourable qualities that reveal themselves as unpleasant attitudes. I always remember Polonius's last precept to his departing son Laertes,

> This above all, – to thy own self be true;
> And it must follow, as the night the day,
> Thou can'st not then be false to any man.
> (William Shakespeare, *Hamlet*, I.3.80)

Early Christian theology defined the Seven Deadly Sins as pride, envy, anger, sloth, avarice, gluttony and lust. These are always our stumbling blocks in any generation, though at any one time one or more of them may predominate. At the moment I would place pride, avarice and lust before the other four. There are, of course, other serious (I would call them deadly myself) sins as well, but they can be subsumed in the cardinal seven. With pride, for instance, there is also vainglory, haughtiness and a tendency to look down on 'inferior' people (racism comes in here). Envy brings with it dishonesty, an appetite for power and hatred, while anger can easily lead to dishonesty, persecution and murder. One needs to add a caveat that there is also righteous indignation which can sometimes ignite and explode into frank anger. Jesus himself showed this when he went into the Temple and drove out all who were buying and selling in the sacred precincts. He upset the tables of the money-changers and the seats of the dealers in pigeons, and said to them, 'Scripture says, "My house shall be called a house of prayer"; but you are making it a bandits' den' (Matthew 21:12–13). The Old Testament references to Jesus' words are to be found in Isaiah 56:7 and particularly Jeremiah 7:11.

Avarice is a greed of the mind and it is the precursor of all improper desires, especially regarding wealth and power. Gluttony brings with it all manner of physical ailments and a more dangerous type of yearning for material benefits. Lust is clearly lascivious passion with an animal desire for sexual indulgence, but the really interesting sin is sloth.

On a very superficial level sloth could simply be regarded as habitual indolence, and the laziness could be extended to include the toleration of unacceptable social, moral or political attitudes, but the early Christian writers aligned sloth also to melancholy or despair. This combination of sloth (or torpor) and despair is classically called 'accidie'. Here I take issue, because I cannot regard melancholy or despair as sinful as much as symptoms of a severe mental illness known as depression. It is interesting that since my return from the 'portals of death' which happened in June and July 1997, I have had recurrent episodes of mild depression lasting up to three or four weeks. The last of these occurred during my very recent three weeks' holiday in Barbados at the end of February and beginning of March 1998. I now realize that I have always had a depressive tendency which has usually been subtly disguised by my intense capacity for work on an intellectual plane, and therefore I could not be accused of harbouring sloth; but now that I am doing less work in my slow process of recovery (which, thank God, is progressing far better than I dared hope), I have had much more time for inner reflection. Many painful memories of my earlier life are tending to dominate my reflections, and when these emerge they inevitably evoke a mood of depression, fortunately not severe enough to necessitate medication. I have come to know, and here I speak hesitantly realizing that many readers will regard this as sheer self-opinionation, that this is an aspect of the life after death. Indeed, I now know personally, but obviously only subjectively, that what I saw in that terrifying experience is what actually happens to every soul when they die, and the innumerable souls who appeared to be in the Stygian darkness were no delusion but the absolute truth. I now know inwardly that this is hell, which can be described as complete psychical chaos.

However, my view of heaven is less rosy than that described by the theistic religions of the West. It is obviously not a spatial or temporal entity since the soul is no longer incarnate. Heaven is not so much an atmosphere of eternal felicity as one in which the souls who have made a success of earthly life in terms of virtue and hard work mix freely with the great majority of deceased humanity. Their heavenly activity is one of service, inspired by the love of God, in order to bring knowledge and guidance to the great mass of souls in isolated darkness, so that they too may become less isolated and start to coalesce in harmony. In this way I believe they will eventually unite into a mighty host which will be so spiritually educated as to enter as equals and brothers with the 'elect', who are those who have lived decent, productive lives while incarnate. This is the meaning of heaven, where there is complete unity.

There are two further comments that have to be made; the souls of those who have been frankly evil will accept the love of the enlightened ones very gradually, which implies that the heavenly state will be completely timeless. Here we are obviously dealing with a mystery, because during earthly life our activities are completely limited by time and space. It therefore follows that there could be a possibility of further incarnate life of some type after death. The great religions in the East accept reincarnation as an obvious fact, whereas the Western group are dogmatically opposed to the very concept. I feel it is wiser to hold fire and let events show us the way forward. Past-life regression claims do not convince me personally; but I must sympathize with those who feel that on occasion a deep, innate, otherwise completely inexplicable dread might be due to a forgotten past experience of another age which may or may not be hereditary.

It sometimes happens that a criminal may have an elementary sense of integrity: as the saying goes, 'There is honour among thieves'. So much human cruelty has been cunningly concealed beneath the mask of religion. On a lesser plane than evil intent is the virtue of the self-righteous person that serves to occlude their deep-seated distaste for someone of a different colour or race. Racism is surely a deadly sin, and this general attitude of hypocrisy is the converse of integrity. It needs to be confronted and eradicated before one can be within even striking distance of the experience of true happiness. I would have no difficulty in contending that it is preferable to be bad and honest with oneself than good while living an inner lie. On the surface this is, to say the least, highly debatable, until one remembers that the bad person at least knows where they stand, and could, when the full measure of the sinfulness hits them, repent (like the tax-collector in the parable) and seek God's forgiveness. The hypocrite, on the other hand, would remain safely ensconced within the walls of their smug assurance, until some terrible disaster entirely smashed their false world. This would, as likely as not, be the sudden awareness of imminent death, when the conscience is laid completely bare and every memory, together with its moral component, has to be directly confronted.

This, I believe, is basically the judgement that awaits us all when we die; we being ourselves the judge, inasmuch as the living God is immanent in every soul – which includes all

living things. We humans differ from even our more
advanced mammalian relatives in possessing a mind that can
register each moment in time, judging the significance of
each passing event. This capacity for judgement brings with
it enormous responsibility for the welfare of all that builds
up human society. When this way of life dominates one's
thoughts and inspires one's emotions, one's integrity is as a
shining light. Though the person should themself be unaware
of it, they are perfect transmitters of the grace of God. To be
like one of the servants of the Most High is the full manifestation of spirituality as well as its crowning reward; it will
persist, no matter how sordid the circumstances around the
person may be. Indeed, one's very presence illuminates the
environment. The number of people who have attained this
degree of sanctity is, in my experience, not large. But I will
recount the life of someone seven years my senior who is
both a long-standing friend and a true illustration of
integrity.

She comes of Viennese aristocratic stock, and, as one
would expect, of Catholic upbringing. But she made the
fateful decision to marry an eminent Jewish surgeon. With
the advent of the *Anschluss* the Nazis saw to it that both of
them were sent to a nearby concentration camp called Maut-
hausen. He was promptly murdered, but her life was spared
after she had been severely beaten. The injuries that this
torture produced have prevented her kneeling down even
today six decades later. She had one child, a daughter, before
this terrible event, and both of them managed to escape to
England in 1941 at the very peak of the Second World War.

After some years she married an Asian diplomat and
became deeply acquainted with and sympathetic towards
Buddhism. She found that through the teaching of the
Enlightened One a deeper understanding of Christianity
came to her. In due course her second husband also died,
and her daughter, by this time an adult, moved to America.
My friend was then left on her own.

She happened to attend a lecture which I was delivering,
and soon a mutual contact of like souls developed. She

found that my manner of delivery as well as the content of its message accorded almost identically with that of her second husband. We met 28 years ago, and our friendship has deepened into one of the few really gratifying experiences of my life.

Her integrity has been made clear to me by her accepting the various vicissitudes of her life, not merely graciously but by positively growing through them. They have not changed her so much as deepened her innate spirituality in the process of imbibing the wisdom and tradition of two major religions apart from Christianity as well as confronting her with treasurable aspects of Islam and Hinduism. She is a friend of numerous younger people of varying shades of belief and has the capacity of drawing out the best aspects of that belief. Her attitude towards religion is universalistic, and in the words of Terence, no human being is alien to her.

On the other hand, she has little sympathy towards the permissive society, while being innately hostile to any form of personal discrimination. This has obviously grown through her own experience as a victim of Hitlerism, but I suspect that it has always been in her.

My last thought concerns fate and destiny. Being personal once more and I hope forgivably so, for a book of this type loses much of its message if one excludes personal experience from its pages, I have no doubt that destiny formed my life before I was born. Jeremiah was told 'Before I formed you in the womb I chose you, and before you were born I consecrated you, I appointed you a prophet to the nations' (Jeremiah 1:5). In my case I knew even as a small boy that I would never marry, and my whole outlook as a child and adolescent was that of a mature adult; in Chapter 7 I spoke about speaking to God when I was a small child. In a peculiar way I have never really been young at all; only now as a man of 70 have I had the first proper holiday in 25 years, albeit for only three weeks, in a life full of work, mostly for other people – and I write this with neither pride nor regret but as a matter of fact.

I did not choose Christianity, because my spirituality is

essentially universalistic – this is what brought my friend and
me so closely together and so rapidly too. But it was decreed
that I should embrace Christianity and I followed in complete obedience, despite the fact that neither Christian history
nor the Christians I knew personally were especially inspiring. Indeed, if one meditates dispassionately on two millennia of Christian history, the good and the bad elements are
almost equivalent in power, yet I did what was required of
me, and I do not regret my obedience either. The teachings
of Jesus are beyond compare. The only problem, as with
numerous other spiritual teachings, is their impracticability
for common humanity. If only we could follow the precepts
of the Sermon on the Mount (Matthew 5–7) the world
would be as the heaven described in theistic religion. But
how many millennia will have to pass before this wonderful
state materializes? Nevertheless I, as a mere nobody, was
called on to practise preaching, writing, deliverance work
(exorcism) and counselling as a Christian minister.

Now at the end of my career I can see exactly why it had
to be; I was given a perfect platform for enunciating eternal
truths and to a very limited extent, even living them. This
ought to apply in their own particular way to every minister
whether Christian or belonging to some other great faith. It
is on people like me and them that the ultimate survival of
humanity depends, but the temptation towards self-aggrandizement and power can be insurmountable unless, like me,
one has an innate sense of low esteem. Alfred Adler might
describe this as an inferiority complex; it can certainly be
crippling if not directly confronted, but it is also essential if
one is to do God's work properly. The really great world
teachers, especially Gautama and Jesus, have shown this
humility perfectly and the same would broadly apply to Lao
Tzu, Confucius and Zoroaster.

So, therefore, my Christian ministry was not an attempt
at escaping from Jewish stigmatization, remembering Shy-
lock's well-merited rebuke 'For suff'rance is the badge of all
our tribe' (*The Merchant of Venice*, I.3.108), since I did not
change my ultra-Jewish surname, Israel, into something more

'Aryan' (as my parents advised me to do before I came to England). Rather, I fulfilled a destiny which was pre-arranged, regarding myself as neither better nor worse than other people. I do not see myself as a convert; indeed, the very concept of enforced conversion, even on an emotional level, revolts me – this may spring from the memory of a previous persecution in a past life, for all I know.

This brings me to a final thought about destiny and fate. Destiny is a power that appears to foreordain a person's life. I have previously quoted Freud's statement that anatomy is destiny, and this would certainly be true in my case because I was born with very flat feet; these were the basis of my inadequacy in playing games and hence were a cause of my unpopularity in my youth. To this, of course, was added the prevalent anti-Semitism of that period in South Africa. But all was not lost, because the isolation consequent on this and also my being an only child forced me to develop my intellect. St Paul puts it so beautifully when he writes 'As we know, all things work together for good for those who love God' (Romans 8:28). Were it not for my unhappiness I could not have fulfilled my destiny, and indeed this was part of my destiny.

I believe that we all have a destiny, though few of us are even aware of it and certainly do nothing to actualize it. Most people's thoughts are centred solely on material objectives like gaining money or achieving power and personal success. Even these are acceptable motives if used for a noble purpose, but usually they are merely items of personal status. Fate, on the other hand, is a power that decides the final outcome of an event such as a person's life and death. We are bound to live our lives within a compass of personal destiny and appointed fate. What is prepared after our death we will know at the decreed time.

Though I am sympathetic to the concepts of destiny and fate, I have to add a caveat; on their own they lack a moral component. For instance, if I were tempted to steal and yielded accordingly, the subsequent punishment would be part of my destiny. If, on the other hand, I was able to resist that temptation that would likewise have been an aspect of my destiny. Free will to any significant extent would therefore be annulled by the Higher Power that had already decreed not only my character but also the way in which I responded to the difficulties that my personality had precipitated. I believe that God has, as it were, given us the tools pertinent to our particular personality, but how we use them is very much our own choice. Therefore, destiny has a strongly foreordained aspect, but how it develops and grows depends on our individual response to the challenges that life in its fullness presents to us.

Shakespeare puts it thus in the mouth of Brutus in *Julius Caesar*, (IV.3.216–19):

> There is a tide in the affairs of men
> Which, taken at the flood, leads on to fortune;
> Omitted, all the voyage of their life
> Is bound in shallows and in miseries.

Enlightenment

Enlightenment occurs when one's consciousness is suddenly illuminated by the Divine light and one understands something that was previously obscure. It was seen literally in the case of the man born blind to whom Jesus restored the gift of sight. The Pharisees, however, were furious because of Jesus' unorthodox religious practice (and also, of course, from intense jealousy) and were out to prove that this could not have been so, either that he was not the same man, or else he was the subject of gross deception. The Pharisees insisted that a sinner like Jesus could not possibly have worked a miracle of any type. As the controversy raged the blind man's parents were summoned, and when they had been questioned, they replied,

> 'We know that he is our son, and that he was born blind. But how it is that he can now see, or who opened his eyes, we do not know. Ask him; he is of age; let him speak for himself.' His parents gave this answer because they were afraid of the Jews;

the Jewish authorities had already agreed that anyone who acknowledged Jesus as the Messiah should be banned from the synagogue; that is why his parents said, 'He is of age; ask him.' So for the second time they summoned the man who had been blind and said, 'Speak the truth before God. We know that this man is a sinner.' 'Whether or not he is a sinner I do not know,' the man replied. 'All I know is this: I was blind and now I can see.'

(John 9:18–25)

It is interesting that we often use the verb 'see' in the context of understanding as well as its usual visual application. The Buddha (which means the Enlightened One) had one of the most celebrated experiences of enlightenment. He was surely born ready to receive enlightenment, but his illumination occurred only when he was a young man. Being the son of a king, he was protected from all knowledge of the dark side of life until he ventured forth beyond the confines of his family's domain, and came face to face with a person decrepit with age, one who was very ill, and finally one who had just died. So great an impression did these three inevitable components of life make upon him that he left his kingdom with his wife and small son. He sought instead to know the truth, visiting various teachers, all wise men in the Hindu tradition, and from them he heard much traditional wisdom. But he still was floundering. One day, whilst sitting under a tree, his mind was suddenly illuminated with Divine reality. He realized that all life is suffering, and the way to conquer suffering is by eliminating all personal desire. The culmination is what is known as the Noble Eightfold Path of Buddhism: Right Understanding, Right Thought, Right Speech, Right Action, Right Livelihood, Right Effort, Right Mindfulness, Right Concentration. He tried various austerities, all to no avail, so he realized the ideal of the Middle Way to attaining the Noble Eightfold Path.

In the Christian tradition the great example of enlightenment is St Paul's (Saul of Tarsus) conversion to Christianity; in Acts 8:1 Saul was among those who approved of the protomartyr Stephen's execution, and in Acts 8:3 he is reported as harrying the Church, entering house after house, seizing men and women and sending them to prison. In Acts 9 Saul, still breathing murderous threats against the Lord's disciples, went to the high priest and applied for letters to the synagogues at Damascus authorizing him to arrest any followers of the new way whom he found, men or women, and bring them to Jerusalem. While he was still on the road and nearing Damascus, suddenly a light from the sky flashed all around him.

> He fell to the ground and heard a voice saying, 'Saul, Saul, Why are you persecuting me?' 'Tell, me Lord,' he said, 'who you are.' The voice answered, 'I am Jesus, whom you are persecuting. But now get up and go into the city, and you will be told what you have to do.' Meanwhile the men who were travelling with him stood speechless; they heard the voice but could see no one. Saul got up from the ground, but when he opened his eyes he could not see; they led him by the hand and brought him into Damascus. He was blind for three days, and took no food or drink.
>
> (Acts 9:1–9)

It was another disciple named Ananias who, again under Divine instruction, went to Saul and laid his hands on him after which it was as if scales had fallen from his eyes and he regained his sight. He got up and was baptized, and when he had eaten his strength returned (Acts 9:10–19). The people in Damascus were amazed that someone who was so virulently against the faith had changed into its great champion, and soon it became imperative that Saul should leave Damascus and return to Jerusalem. The apostles, needless to say, were distrustful, considering Saul's previous antipathy to the new faith, and it was only through Barnabas, a Cypriot Levite, who had sold an estate which he owned and given the money to the apostles (Acts 4:36–37), that Paul was accepted by the eleven. This was the beginning of his amazing missionary work; indeed, without St Paul it is very doubtful whether the faith that was to be called Christianity would have ever survived at all.

I wonder why the eleven surviving apostles were not

chosen by God for extensive missionary work. The answer lies quite obviously in Paul's great intelligence, the power of his endeavour and his great courage. I could not, however, call him a natural mystic because of his intense hatred against the disciples before his own conversion; a natural mystic has an innate love which would simply be incompatible with the fury of murderous intent that Saul showed before his conversion. But with his conversion a latent mystical tendency became increasingly obvious as is seen in many of his magnificent letters. In other words, when he came close to God he became increasingly aware of the Divine nature presiding in his own soul. Something of the fanatic remained in him, and this is rather a pity when one considers, for instance, the anti-Jewish outbursts in Romans 9–11. But then he frequently softens, and sees the favoured Jews who have become Christians as the 'remnant' mentioned on more than one occasion in the pages of the Old Testament.

Enlightenment can also occur on a secular occasion when a person suddenly sees the truth. Archimedes (287–212 BC) provides a celebrated example. He had a great scientific mind among the ancient Greeks, and was on one occasion presented with a royal crown for his assessment; was it made of gold or simply a counterfeit? He was not allowed to tamper with it. Suddenly, when in his bath, the answer came to him in a flash. The amount of water displaced by the crown would be equal to its weight – if it were composed of an inferior metal its weight would be similar to that of an object of similar appearance made of an alloy of cheaper metals. He was so excited with this enlightenment that he ran down the street shouting 'Eureka!', which means 'I have found'.

Each advance in human understanding has come through the Spirit of God illuminating the mind of a predestined person. This may be a scientific discovery in the fields of technology or medicine, a creative delight in the realm of the arts, or a sudden thrust that initiates a fresh endeavour to philanthropic action amongst the many marginalized members of the world community. At present these include vast populations of fugitives who have been expelled from their homes by evil regimes and had the good fortune not to be killed. Other groups who need constant assistance are the blind, the deaf, the impoverished aged, abused children and those with chronic mental disease. The numerous charities that exist to meet the needs of these people (and also ill-treated animals) had their beginnings in the minds of enlightened individuals, whose imagination has extended far beyond their personal comfort to embrace all humanity, indeed, all life in our great ecosystem.

Truth and beauty

'Beauty is truth, truth beauty', – that is all
Ye know on earth, and all ye need to know.
(John Keats, *Ode on a Grecian Urn*)

Beauty transcends the rational faculty whereby truth is assessed in terms of a collection of verifiable facts. When beauty enlightens the eye, the ear or the mind itself, it carries us to the frontiers of transcendental awareness where the Divine presence is known.

This knowledge is far beyond mere intelligence; it is the unitive knowledge described in the Bible when a chosen husband and wife come together and a child of promise is conceived – a good example is the aged couple Abraham and Sarah begetting Isaac.

The great artists carry their fellows to the knowledge of God by the glory of their beautiful creation. Rembrandt, for example, carries us to the Divine as he depicts the human form. Mozart opens up an eternity of beauty in which musical form is illuminated by the tragicomedy of everyday human life. The greatest of all, in my opinion, is Shakespeare, whose plays and sonnets leave no aspect of human nature unexplored. When we fail most dismally in our

endeavours we are closest to the ultimate truth which is
God.

Let us return once again to the *Ode on a Grecian Urn*:

> Heard melodies are sweet, but those unheard
> Are sweeter; therefore, ye soft pipes, play on;
> Not to the sensual ear, but, more endear'd,
> Pipe to the spirit ditties of no tone.

11 The quest for happiness

This book is concerned with achieving happiness, but most of its contents have shown how very difficult it is to attain this end. The things that seem to be the most desirable in one's life usually turn out to be illusions because they take over one's life and imprison one in a particular aspect of desire. How right the Buddha was when he saw that personal desire was the ultimate cause of suffering but, on the other hand, without desire nothing could ever be achieved. All depends on the nature of the desire and one's way of responding to it.

Happiness is essentially a state of mind where there is a steady contentment with one's lot, whether in good fortune or in bad. The foundation is always spiritual strength and it is achieved only after deep inner searching and experience. Speaking personally, I began to understand the real meaning of happiness only after the terrifying experience I had last year; as I have already explained, it was shown to me that all shall be well in the end, and that it had to be as it was. My part in my life's work has been, and is to be, living as faithfully to myself and the world as I can. I see myself as living on borrowed time and am forced to conclude that there is still work to be done. My holiday in Barbados was marvellous in removing me from my perpetual routine of working, eating and sleeping, with only occasional weekend breaks in the country. Only when this routine was completely broken, even for three weeks, did I consider other aspects of my life.

As I lay on the beach I saw people in bathing costumes, as

I was myself, walking confidently into the sea and I was filled with envy; not only did I admire their strong, confident posture and the handsomeness of young people, but my gaze always fixed a little of the time on their feet: these were not flat but had wonderfully raised arches, as do those of my carer Cliff. Actually my deformity is quite painful if there is no carpet underfoot (as occurred in the hotel in Barbados), but a pair of efficient arch-supports (insoles) makes walking relatively comfortable. I would never before then have believed that I harboured one of the seven deadly sins, but now I have to acknowledge that more than one has afflicted me, though to my credit I believe it has not protruded too visibly externally!

More recently, when people who attended my church or the retreats that I conducted have visited me, they have let me know, quite incidentally, how very irritable I was when people interrupted my flow of inspirational speaking. This applied particularly to retreat conducting, because in church the address is relatively short and one is supported by a choir. It is amazing that until then I did not realize how irascible I could be; indeed, I harboured the illusion that I was rather gentle and mild. It would indeed be scarcely possible for someone speaking under inspiration not to become irritated when people behaved discourteously, but if I had had a finer character, I would have learnt to bear this much more graciously. I must say, however, in mitigation that this tendency to irritability is often a product of the ageing process; no doubt the great saints of religion have been able to curb it effectively but nearly all of them have been lovingly supported by communities of which they were members.

All this goes to show how essential an ingredient a sense of humour is in attaining a fairly constant happiness. As happens so often in the spiritual life, it is our foibles that are our way to perfection, whereas our strengths become weaknesses until they are completely demolished. There is indeed hope for even the least of us, while trying too hard is a certain way to disillusionment.

Happiness does not depend on having anything at all, but on being what one is meant to be. It results when the personality is at peace with itself and in harmony with its surroundings. Wealth, power, friendship, intimate love and especially health are all vital ingredients, but few can be relied on for permanency. This is certainly true of health; the ageing process inevitably brings with it disorders of one system or another. In my case it is the central nervous system that has borne the brunt of my later years with epilepsy and Parkinson's disease, but I might quite as easily have had coronary arterial occlusion, chronic bronchitis and emphysema or diseases of the stomach, bowels, liver or kidneys, to say nothing of peripheral vascular disease, a stroke or cancer. I have had enough hospitalization recently to flinch from any more, but what will be, will be, whether I like it or not, for I have no death wish.

From all this rather autobiographical reflection one can see that the quest for happiness is usually not fulfilled because the person strains for the monumental while ignoring the blessings that surround them day by day. Of course it could be argued that many people in the world live below subsistence level and are doomed to disease and death from the very time of their birth. This is a fact of life that has to be confronted directly, and happiness cannot be attained in a real way until there is political justice in all the countries of the world. Why some people seem to be so highly privileged materially, whereas others slowly starve to death is at least partly a mystery. It depends on the location of the person's birth as well as their parents' disposition. What I would be like now had my mother been less neurotic and quarrelsome and had I not been severely ill-treated by a nurse when I was scarcely out of babyhood, God alone knows. But what matters ultimately is the way in which I have used these particular adversities, which are pretty mild to say the least in a world of indescribably terrible suffering. On the other hand, before I become too self-deprecatory, I have to remember my extreme psychic sensitivity; I can 'pick up' other people's emotions as easily as a magnet attracts iron filings. This is indeed the basis of my deliverance work, and, believe me, this is not the privilege that many people suppose it to be. Had I been more 'normal' I would not have been burdened with this ability. But look at the amount of good that has come out of it for other people, even if I have not particularly benefited from it myself! I believe in fact that the remarkable episode of unconsciousness that I had last year could have been at least partly attributable to psychic attack. Most professional workers would deride this and even regard me as slightly off-centre, while a few ultra-rationalists would say quite frankly that I was mad.

In these pages I have said some rather harsh things about conventional religion, but even more noxious is a dominant type of rationalism that is so extreme as to find no place for anything that cannot be proven directly by the means of science. It is here that great art finds its use in leading us to the right mindfulness of which the Buddha speaks. I have no doubt that there is more to life and death than that which is accepted by pure reason. A deeper power of the soul is necessary before we can know even the reality of the self. From this knowledge we are able to effect a deeper understanding of other mortals and indeed of life in general. Now at last we are in contact with the source of ultimate reality which is one of the many ways in which God, the indescribable, may be approached. The light that surrounded the Buddha and blinded the physical and intellectual faculties of St Paul, albeit temporarily, is the classical manifestation of God. God is light, and in him there is no darkness at all (1 John 1:5). This light cleanses the personality of all its defects, and makes it one with God whose nature embraces all gender as well as race and religion.

When this ultimate truth not only becomes part of our understanding but eventually transforms our character we shall know happiness of a very exalted order. In this state joy may be subsumed. Joy is by no means alien to ordinary people like you and me: there is a sudden rise of consciousness to a peak of realization of the splendour that embraces all creation. We know joy that lasts when we have transcended self-interest completely in service to an activity devoted to the common good. We have in fact to lose our life in the manner of Matthew 10: 39 which we considered in Chapter 6, to know an authentic existence whose centre is God. In the Divine light there is perpetual joy.

Now we have ceased to be isolated individuals but are part of a vast concourse of life. Joy is innocent of all illusions nor does it expect anything, inasmuch as it contains everything. This is the sort of heaven I would expect when every living creature, past, present and future, will have attained joy of this immensity. 'Perfectly to will what God wills, to want what he wants, is to have joy; but if one's will is not quite in unison with God's, there is no joy' (Meister Eckhart, *Talks of Instruction* No 23).

A final qualification. How does all this fit in with the undeniable fact of evil both in ourselves and in the greater world? I am reminded of an observation by Friedrich von Logau (*Sinngedichte* 3,2,24, translated by Henry Wadsworth Longfellow).

> Through the mills of God grind slowly,
> Yet they grind exceeding small;
> Though with patience he stands waiting,
> With exactness grinds he all.

I feel the last word is that which was revealed to Julian of Norwich in the 27th chapter of *Revelation of Divine Love*.

> After this the Lord brought to my mind the longing that I had to Him afore. And I saw that nothing letted me but sin. And so I looked, generally, upon us all, and methought: *if sin had not been, we should all have been clean and like to our Lord, as he made us.*
>
> But Jesus, who in this Vision informed me of all that is needful to me, answered by this word and said: *It behoved that there should be sin; but all shall be well, and all shall be well, and all manner of thing shall be well.*

She saw that the pain that follows committing a sin purges us; it makes us know ourselves and ask for mercy. For the Passion of our Lord is a comfort to us against all this, and so is his blessed will. She saw in these words a marvellous high mystery hid in God which he will open to us in heaven. In other words, sin does help us, or at least the great majority of us, to attain a fully adult stature in our life. Until we have erred we cannot know forgiveness, (as is memorably illustrated in Luke 7: 36–50 where Jesus chides a judgemental Pharisee) and then we can understand and forgive those who have injured us. Now we can grasp that part of the Lord's Prayer which asks that we may be forgiven for our sins as we forgive those who sin against us. It is for this reason that life is essential for the full growth of the person, and why I personally could not imagine for one moment that the process of life is terminated when the body dies. As I have said before, nobody knows the sequel though there are many speculations about this topic. As I was told during my period of semi-consciousness last year, our great work is to live perfectly in the present and let the future take care of itself. Indeed, the future is largely determined by our present attitudes and actions.

Some of my friends object vehemently to the thought of a person like Hitler being able to attain a knowledge of heaven, and I sympathize greatly with them. But I also know that this is an inadequate response to the love of God who, as St Peter was shown, has no favourites (Acts 10: 34). This realization came after the well-disposed centurion Cornelius was directed by a holy angel to send some servants to Peter's home in Joppa, and hear what he had to say. So Peter asked them in and gave them a night's lodging. Next day he set out with them, accompanied by some members of the congregation at Joppa, and on the following day arrived at Caesarea. Cornelius was expecting them and he called together his relatives and close friends. When Peter arrived, Cornelius came to meet him, and bowed to the ground in deep reverence. But Peter raised him to his feet and said 'Stand up; I am only a man like you'. Still talking with him he went in and found a large gathering. He said to them 'I need not tell you that a Jew is forbidden by his religion to visit or associate with anyone of another race. Yet God has shown me clearly that I must not call anyone profane or unclean; that is why I came here without demur when you sent for me. May I ask you what was your reason for doing so?' Cornelius recounted the appearance of the angel and then Peter began: 'I now understand how true it is that God has no favourites, but that in every nation those who are god-fearing and do what is right are acceptable to him'. Shortly before their arrival Peter had had a vision of something that looked like a great sheet full of 'unclean beasts' being lowered to him and him being commanded to take and eat them. This was against strict Jewish law, needless to say. At last the interpretation of the dream became obvious to him; it was a preparation for the reception of the first Gentiles into the Christian fold (Acts 10).

Coming back to the question of Hitler entering the heaveny state, it is matter primarily of Divine grace and also a thoroughly repentant Adolf Hitler. This second proviso must be emphasized, otherwise any concept of morality would fly out of the window. Love flourishes only in an atmosphere of truth, otherwise gross hypocrisy prevails. This is the reason why I distrust 'good' people so much, for they do tend to look down on those whom they regard as inferior. Indeed, until we can separate our illusions from the truth about ourselves, we will be living in a state of false security that has nothing to do with happiness. We ought not to have happiness as a right as some protagonists currently insist. It is earned by the way we give of ourselves to life, especially our fellow humans. In the giving lies the happiness.

The proof of any happiness that I may have, even at this moment, is evidenced by the happiness that others acquire through my presence, whether in person or by my writings. It is on this level that this very book has to be judged. If all books could be considered in terms of the harvest of the Spirit that St Paul writes about in Galatians 5: 22–23 (love, joy, peace, patience, kindness, goodness, fidelity, gentleness and self-control), the human race would be accorded an immeasurable service.

> If there be righteousness in the heart,
> there will be beauty in the character.
> If there is beauty in the character
> there will be harmony in the home.
> If there is harmony in the home,
> there will be order in the nation.
> When there is order in each nation
> there will be peace in the world.
>
> (Very old Chinese proverb)

Envoi

What a strange person I appear to be; an ethnic Jew, a Christian priest, and a spiritual univeralist. I am indeed catholic in the true sense of the word, which means universal. Though a Jew, and having had all my relatives in Lithuania exterminated by the Germans, I still find it repugnant that Jews, now having acquired an independent state of their own, should be the agents of dispossession of their Palestinian neighbours. With the amazing sequence of events in South Africa and the growing friendship between various racial groups I look with equal hope towards an Israeli–Arab reconciliation.

This is what God was reported to have said to Moses,

> You yourselves have seen what I did to Egypt and how I have carried you on eagles' wings and brought you here to me. If only you will now listen to me and keep my covenant, then out of all peoples you will become my special possession; for the whole earth is mine. You will be to me a kingdom of priests, my holy nation.
>
> (Exodus 19: 4–6)

Though no fundamentalist myself, I accept these words literally. The contribution of the Jews to world civilization has been of incredible magnitude (not least of all two other major religions, Christianity and Islam), so incredible that it has been an important factor in their perpetual persecution.

If one is chosen by God it means, as my whole life has taught me so eloquently, service, suffering and sacrifice.

There is no personal glory at all in it, but the reward is bringing all people to human actualization, the end of which is happiness. I believe I must be one of the few humans who has seen the other side of death and I know what a great work it is to bring those in darkness into the light. It is interesting that this idea is found in Mahayana Buddhism in the form of the Bodhisattva ideal. The Bodhisattva is one who has become completely enlightened, and having attained Nirvana, and so freed at last from the melancholy wheel of birth and death, renounces his blessedness in order that he may remain to help suffering humanity. In his divine compassion he says, 'for others' sake this reward I yield'. He accomplishes the Great Renunciation and becomes a Saviour of the World. I certainly could not claim this for myself, but the way forward has been obviously indicated in the life I have been destined to experience. It is only when concepts of this magnitude inform humanity that there will be peace on earth and goodwill amongst all that lives.

In my opinion, the Buddha is the great World Teacher, whereas the Christ is the great World Exemplar. What I like particularly about Hinduism and Buddhism is their indifference to proselytism; what I dislike about Christianity and Islam is their ardent desire to make converts. I see this not as a way of enlightening the world so much as one of religious self-aggrandizement. The Jews have erred on the other extreme, at least in the Orthodox tradition, towards rigid exclusiveness – as we remember Peter telling Cornelius. As far as I am concerned the hope of world religion lies in mystical liberalism, a state in which the enlightened mind is illuminated by suprarational mystical love, which is the very essence of God himself. My own endeavours have always been directed by and towards this ideal. Without it I see only destruction ahead, but with it we may begin to see heaven on earth.